ABOUT THE AUTHOR

Dr Dina Glouberman is the visionary co-founder of Skyros Holistic Holidays, in Greece, Thailand, Cambodia and Cuba, author of the classic books *Life Choices, Life Changes* and *The Joy of Burnout* and an international trainer, coach and psychotherapist. She has been a pioneer for over 30 years in creating, teaching and practising the use of Imagework, the groundbreaking process that harnesses the imagination to guide our lives and create positive life choices and profound life changes.

ALSO BY DR DINA GLOUBERMAN

Life Choices, Life Changes: Develop Your Personal Vision with Imagework (Skyros Books, 2010)

Life Choices, Life Changes: CD and MP3 imagery exercise series (5 CDs and 16 MP3s) (http://www.dinaglouberman. com/shop/#cd-list)

The Joy of Burnout: How the End of the World Can Be a New Beginning (Skyros Books, 2007)

You Are What You Imagine: MP3 imagery exercise series (http://www.dinaglouberman.com/shop/#cd-list)

You Are What You Imagine

Dr Dina Glouberman

WATKINS PUBLISHING
LONDON

This edition first published in the UK and USA 2014 by
Watkins Publishing Limited
PO Box 883
Oxford, OX1 9PL
UK

A member of Osprey Group

For enquiries in the USA and Canada:
Osprey Publishing
PO Box 3985
New York, NY 10185-3985
Tel: (001) 212 753 4402
Email: info@ospreypublishing.com

1 3 5 7 9 10 8 6 4 2

Designed and typeset by Creative Plus Publishing Limited
Edited by Dawn Bates
www.creative-plus.co.uk

Printed and bound by CPI Group (UK) Ltd, Croydon, CR0 4YY

A CIP record for this book is available from the British Library

ISBN: 978-1-78028-763-8

Watkins Publishing is supporting the Woodland Trust, the UK's leading
woodland conservation charity, by funding tree-planting initiatives and
woodland maintenance.

www.watkinspublishing.co.uk

To My Soul Community

ACKNOWLEDGEMENTS

Thank you to my students, clients, friends and family, and indeed to all the people who kindly agreed to be interviewed, for your stories which appear in this book, not always with your real names, and for your courage, honesty and companionship that inspires me daily. Thank you to my publisher, Jo Lal of Watkins, for believing that this book will make a difference. Thank you to all my friends and family who have accompanied me on the journey of this book, and especially to Lois Graessle and Ari Andricopoulos, who read early drafts and encouraged me to take this book seriously, and to Kate Daniels and Shakya Kumara, who helped me get started with focus and determination. Thank you to Raymond Aaron, whose course on writing short books taught me how to organize my writing in a new way. Thank you to Ann Hackmann and Valerie Thomas for your wonderful academic work on imagery. Thank you to all the authors whose books have shone a light in dark places.

Thank you, in fact, to all the members of my soul community.

You are all part of this book and of me.

CONTENTS

INTRODUCTION

If you've ever seen the sun rise from the sea, you will have some idea of the magnificence of the journey to a new beginning. Prepare yourself for a great adventure that will engage you on all levels – mind, emotion, body and soul – and that will astound you again and again as you discover how vast are the possibilities of being you.

Please know that if you are willing to embark on this adventure and to stay the course, then no matter how you may feel right now, and how challenging is the way ahead, the moment will certainly come when you look around at your new life and say to yourself with pride and amazement 'Well done!'

The journey is based on three steps.

Your first step is to recognize that your present life situation, however difficult or stuck it may seem, can be the catalyst that gets you moving towards your new life – and to say *Yes* to this journey. Your second step is that inner transformation that can bring you to a turning point, to the moment when you look round a corner and get a new and expanded view of who you are and where you are going. Your third step is to build that turning point vision into a real new beginning and a new life.

Catalyst, turning point and new beginning. Simple. But not necessarily easy.

This is not a fairy-tale journey, and your new reality will not be a happily-ever-after one. But then, you wouldn't believe me if I promised you that. Your new life will include the joy that flows through you, the pain that you accept as part of life, the new successes and new failures, the growing knowledge of who you really are, the discovery of what you really love, the understanding of what you contribute to the world around, indeed the whole package of a life that is constantly renewing itself.

Are you up for this? I hope so. Because this is what this book, and your own imagination, can help you to do. The secret is to learn how to make changes in your imagination before you make them in reality. This is the basis of the Imagework approach I have created and pioneered for over 30 years.

WHAT IS IMAGEWORK?

Everything that you create in your life, from an omelette to a multinational company to a love affair, begins as an image in your mind. These images, which have such a profound effect on your life, are often unconscious and may well originate in very early childhood. It stands to reason that some of them will be long past their sell-by date, and may be leading you somewhere you don't want to go. If so, isn't it time to bring them up to date?

Imagework is a safe and empowering way to harness your imagination to guide your life and create positive life choices and profound life changes. It will enhance and transform every aspect of your inner and outer life – personally, professionally, creatively and spiritually.

Imagework is the ideal tool for this journey to new beginnings because, once you know how to work with them, your images can help you every step of the way. They will show you how to make sense of where you are now and see more clearly where you need to go, and then they will also help you make the right decisions, and carry them through. You couldn't ask for a better companion and guide than your own imagination.

I call this process Imagework rather than visualization because not everyone is visual. Even when I or other people use the term 'visualization', remember that images can be seen, heard, smelled, felt, even tasted, and the fact that you may not be able literally to see a clear inner picture doesn't really matter. I'm not visual myself, so I know.

I've been working with images and teaching Imagework for as long as I can remember and I've never met anyone who couldn't experience and use images. Rest assured that you won't be the first!

Imagework is a wonderful tool for therapists, counsellors, coaches, consultants, facilitators, doctors, healers, spiritual teachers, and indeed anyone who works with people and wants to help clients get to the heart of the matter and find a new way forward. But it is also a self-help method, designed to bring the secrets of all these professionals direct to you via your own imagination.

Creating it was my way of saying that although I love working with people therapeutically, and I know I really can make a difference, in the long run I would prefer to be a teacher. I want to give you the skills you need so that you can access your own wisdom, love and power, and think and act differently every day of your life.

IS THIS BOOK FOR YOU?

- ◆ Do the words 'difficult times', 'turning points' or 'new beginnings' ring bells for you?
- ◆ Are you facing challenging or painful life events without a clear end in sight? Or are you feeling stuck in a rut? Or are you perhaps yearning to embark on something new that you know may be wonderful, but is nevertheless outside your comfort zone?
- ◆ Are you willing to begin to listen to the whispers of your heart and soul and follow them?
- ◆ Does bringing more creativity, fulfilment and joy back into your life feel important enough to do something about it?
- ◆ Is it time for a turning point in your life or work?
- ◆ Could a new beginning be just around the corner?

If the answer to any of these questions is *Yes*, why not read on?

HOW TO READ THIS BOOK

This book is divided into three parts, your three steps:

- ◆ The first part is *Step One: Your Catalyst*. It sketches the pathway from where you are to your new beginnings so that you can see your way forward, and introduces your Imagework tools for the journey. You will also learn how and why the difficult or stuck times you may be in are not only the end of one road, but the beginning of a new one, and hopefully you will say a resounding *Yes* to starting your journey.

♦ The second part is *Step Two: Your Turning Point.* It is about the inner shift in your attitudes that makes a new beginning in your life possible. It includes accepting your present situation and feelings, finding the part of you that is stable when all else fails, expanding to get a bigger picture, and beginning to look round the corner and vision your new future.

♦ The third part is *Step Three: Your New Beginning.* It is about saying *Yes* to your turning point vision, planning and taking the practical steps to build it into your life and eventually creating your new beginning and a balanced joy-filled life.

It is much quicker to read a book than to practise your new skills, and certainly quicker than to make these changes in your life. So do be prepared to read the whole book to get a sense of where you are going, and then to go back and re-read each chapter when the time is right.

YOUR SPIRITUAL GYM

When you want to learn or practise a new physical skill, you may well go to the gym. I want to introduce to you a new kind of gym, the Spiritual Gym.

Is this something religious? No, but it is something to do with the spirit of being you. The Spiritual Gym is where you exercise the skills you need for your life, rather than those you need just for your physical body. It is the inner space in which you can discover, and practise, the ways in which imagery can help you understand yourself and guide your life. It is also where you strengthen your inner muscles, including the ones that help you live truthfully, stay on course, keep your heart open, and generally be aligned with your deepest, truest self. Learning to work with your inner imagery can help you with all of this.

Since you can't run a marathon without doing any training, doesn't it make sense that you need training to develop the inner skills that will help you run your life?

At the end of every chapter you will find a Spiritual Gym imagery exercise that gives you a personal experience of what I have been talking about in the chapter. These exercises are designed to help you find out what is going on for you, what is stopping you, how to get past it, and what your next step might be.

They are probably more important than the chapter, so don't just skip them and go on to the next chapter! The words will help, but they won't train your imagination to be your best friend. Only you can do that. The secret, as always, is practice, practice, practice.

If there is anyone you genuinely trust with whom you can team up to read the book and do the exercises together, that is great. It will encourage you to stay on track and make it more fun. The presence of someone else also enhances imagery and other deep experiences because you can surrender and feel safe in a way that isn't always possible on your own.

There are a few principles that you need to remember when you do any form of imaging. My 8 Tips to Harnessing Your Imagination will help you here (see page 42). My book *Life Choices, Life Changes*,[1] is a fuller introduction to the principles and practice of using imagery to guide you from within. If you want to be guided through the exercises, which is always a lot easier than reading instructions, do go to my website (http://www.dinaglouberman.com/shop/#cd-list) to download MP3s of the imagery exercises. That way, I can talk you – or both you and your buddy – through the exercises. For a fast-track approach you may want to attend a workshop, which offers the powerful and life-changing experience of being facilitated on the path to your new beginnings in the company of like-minded people. You will also be able to set up regular meetings afterwards to keep each other on track. (http://www.dinaglouberman.com/courses-coaching/courses/).

WHY NOT LEARN TO IMAGINE BETTER?

You are, indeed, what you imagine. Is it time to take a risk and expand your possible ways of being you? After all, if where you are is the best you've been able to imagine, and if it leaves something to be desired, why not learn to imagine better?

A NEW BEGINNING

Educating your imagination is your single most important tool to understand and guide your life, and this is particularly so when you are about to turn a corner. By the time you finish this book, I hope you will not only have a new vision of where you are, where you are going, and how to get there, but also a new way of thinking that will illuminate your life in the years to come.

That in itself is a new beginning.

STEP ONE:

YOUR CATALYST

CHAPTER 1

Seeing Your Way to a New Beginning

Good books often start with a story, and this book is no exception. My story is about a great man, the late Chad Varah. You may not have heard of him, but you may well have heard of the organization he created.

Chad Varah was the inspiring British Anglican priest who founded the Samaritans, an organization that offers free round-the-clock, non-religious telephone support to people who are feeling distressed, despairing or suicidal. It was the world's first crisis hotline organization and is still the leading one.

In the early 1990s, I published a series of articles about life turning points.[1] I had the opportunity to interview a wide range of prominent writers, actors, politicians and thought leaders and to ask them about the turning points in their lives. They included Tariq Ali, Tony Benn, Robert Bly, Shakti Gawain, Lynne Franks, Gabrielle Roth, DM Thomas, Chad Varah and Michael York; you will find some of their stories in this book. Chad Varah told me this story about the time a shocking suicide paved the way towards this wonderful organization, which has saved countless lives around the world:

The biggest turning point came after my ordination. I had to report at my parish in Lincoln. I arrived at the vicarage by bicycle, and the vicar's wife all flustered

met me at the door.
She said, 'I'm glad you've got your bicycle. The vicar's
come down with 'flu. Can you get down to St Peter's in
Eastgate in less than ten minutes and take a funeral?'

Young Chad Varah peddled down there, still wearing his college robes, and discovered that the funeral was for a 13-year-old girl. He couldn't understand why he was being taken to unconsecrated ground, until he was told that the girl had to be buried there because it was a suicide.

'You're not telling me she committed suicide at 13,'
I asked, shocked.
'Yes, sir.'
'Why?'
'Well we don't know, do we? But in this case it so
happens that she went to the same school as my
daughter. She told my daughter that she'd started
bleeding between her legs and was very upset about
it. My daughter didn't know what it was either. She
hadn't had it.'
I was really shattered. It was pissing with rain, but I
stayed there and made a vow to the little girl I never
knew who changed my life.
I vowed, 'I shall educate children of your age about
sex, even if I get called a dirty old man at the age of
24.' That very night in the church in Eastgate, I began.[2]

SEEING YOUR WAY
For Chad Varah, the path from a difficult moment to a

new beginning seemed almost instantaneous. Shocked at the fact that a young girl felt she had to commit suicide because she didn't know simple facts about her own body, and armed with the memory of an old Bishop who had freed him by telling him about sex when he was very young, he saw the danger of failing to educate children about their bodies. He stood there in the rain to make the vow that would change his life – and of course many other lives – and he began to teach that very evening.

This rather brief event actually includes the three steps we all have to go through to begin anew:

- The catalyst: The event or experience or challenge that changes your life and starts you moving.
- The turning point: The insight or inner expansion or vision that puts the catalyst into a bigger picture, sheds a new light on it and on you, and shows you a way forward.
- The new beginning: Saying *Yes* to this turning point and building it into your life in a positive and usually external way by taking some kind of action.

Chad Varah's catalyst was the information about the young girl's suicide. His turning point was the (implicit) understanding that a culture that doesn't educate children about sex is potentially lethal and that he had to do what he could to change that. His oath was his resounding *Yes* to his role in making this happen, and the new beginning came when he started teaching that evening.

Of course, he didn't stop there. As he described it:

One thing led to another. From teaching children I went on to give sex talks to those about to be married, which was unheard of in those days. I gradually became known as a sex therapist and began to be asked to write articles on sex. In 1954, 18 years later, I was Vicar of Clapham Junction and an article I wrote caused over 235 people to consult me about their sexual problems, of whom 12 per cent were suicidal. Ever the scientist, I asked myself what kind of help could have saved them… I decided the only thing to do was to ask the suicidal themselves…

Rather amazingly, he decided to use the media to let it be known that he was available at any time, day or night, on the telephone or face-to-face, to help suicidal people to talk through their problems.

I did try to get out of this terrible commitment by saying to God, 'I'm as busy as a one-armed juggler with this parish. I couldn't possibly do this 24-hour-a-day stuff. I would need to be rector of a church in the City of London where there are practically no inhabitants. So don't look at me.'

Two weeks later, out of the blue, I was offered this parish in the City!

When the telephone number he wanted for this service, MAN 9000, turned out to be the newly connected telephone number in his church, Chad Varah told me this:

'Stop it,' I said to God. 'This is getting spooky.'

I started to offer this service on 2 November, 1953, with only my secretary to help me… Eventually volunteers gathered round, as well as people seeking help… Within seven years of starting up and discovering the right way of running the Samaritans, people in other countries were taking up the idea.

The path from difficult moments to new beginnings does not always show itself so clearly as it did to this extraordinary man, and when you can't see the way forward, it is easy to give up early on and not stay the course. This is why it is so helpful to know the road signs to look for and see 'the light at the end of the tunnel'. It can keep you on track when you might otherwise lose hope.

I am reminded of a time, some years ago, when I got a third-degree burn on my leg. I had stepped off a rather old motorcycle on the wrong side and hit the exhaust pipe. I was directing and teaching on a Skyros holiday session[3] and, as it happened, among the participants there were a few doctors. One of them kindly took charge of showing me how to clean the wound, cover it with whatever I needed to kill the infection, dress it and so on. I was grateful. But the wound just did not get better. I won't go into the gory details about how awful it was.

One day, I was walking down the hill in tears, feeling that this wound was never going to heal, and I happened to meet another one of the doctors, a lovely Welsh woman with a soft accent. She saw me crying and I told her what was happening. 'How will this ever get better?' I asked, hopelessly.

She answered my question absolutely literally. She told me how it would start at one corner, and how it would proceed with the healing process.

Perhaps it was just nature taking its course, but to me it felt as if my healing began from that moment. Why? Now, I could literally see the end of it. And if you can imagine it, you can become it.

The purpose of this chapter, therefore, is to give you a little map, so that you too can see the end of these difficult times, and the process whereby you will arrive at new beginnings. This will make the journey so much easier.

Do you think the butterfly forming in the cocoon knows on some level that all these changes are part of a plan? I hope so.

TURNING POINTS

In a sense, the beginning and end of this process are fairly obvious. There is the catalyst, the event that gets you going because your old life doesn't really work anymore, and the new beginning, which marks the beginning of your new life.

But there is a crucial step in the middle, the one I referred to above as the turning point. While the catalyst and the new beginning both tend to involve external change, the turning point is the inner change or insight that gives you a new view of your past, present and future. It is what enables you to turn your catalyst into a new beginning.

My friend Stuart was telling me about his journey from clinical depression and cancer to a new beginning. For him the turning point was the awareness that he needed to strip away whatever attitudes, thoughts and feelings were not really his own, or were from the past, let go of his definition of himself as mentally ill or faulty goods, and then step by step delineate the core passions that had consistently been part of who he was. As he put it, 'I was able to distil the elements that actually made up my life.' This seemed worth getting out of bed for.

A turning point is a fundamental shift in your attitudes, a willingness to open up and listen to yourself and to life in a new way. It is always some kind of expansion; you move out of what is often a very closed down contracted place, get a bigger picture of what life means to you, and out of that bigger picture get a new sense of what your next step might be.

It is important to remember that this is not about your outer life but your inner life. You can travel the world, have a new job or relationship or home every year, and yet within you are still same old, same old. Or you can profoundly recommit to the life you already have and approach everything differently without changing a thing on a practical level and that may be a turning point.

Usually that bigger picture is not just a personal one. When Chad Varah makes that vow in the rain, this is very obvious. But even if it looks as if you are personally deciding about your own life, on some level you are making a decision also about the nature of who you really are and what life is really about.

It has some element of a bigger awareness, of what it is like to be human, or what your soul is whispering, or what life is asking of you, or what you might be here to learn, or what your passion is, or what you can offer to others, or

22

what limits you need to transcend in order to be more fully yourself. It is one step in a lifelong path towards becoming closer and closer to a life that fully expresses your purpose, joy, love, indeed your life force.

Stuart realized that his understandings and his passions were not only his own path to recovery, but could be routes to health and wellbeing for others. He is now working as a community organizer specializing in whole-person recovery from substance misuse. He is incredibly successful in this role, and absolutely loves doing it.

Every difficult time you go through gives you the opportunity for an expansion. I am not saying that difficult times are good for you and you should have more of them. I am only saying that if you are having a difficult time, you can also turn it into some kind of blessing.

When you begin to value expansion for its own sake, and you can see that each expansion takes you closer to where you want to go in life, expansion can become your intention and your habitual choice. Then you don't need times to be difficult for you to want to have more and more turning points.

After all, the entire universe is expanding, so doesn't it make sense that we humans, microcosms of the macrocosm, are expanding too?

Once you have a turning point, you need to ground it in the world, as Chad Varah did. This is your new beginning. Without this, you can be in trouble.

And this is the health warning I always give: If you become aware of what your path is, and you don't follow it, you are in more trouble than if you had remained unconscious. This is why you can suffer so much from missing a turning point that is calling to you, or from failing to follow through with a new beginning. In fact, this, in my view, is what burnout is all about.[4]

Is it always in this order?

This three-step process of catalyst to turning point to new beginning doesn't always come in that order. Sometimes, for example, the first step of coming out of your difficult times is simply to do something new and keep doing it no matter how you feel. This simple persistence can be a new beginning that opens you up to a new sense of life, which is of course a turning point. Stuart found that caring for his new baby forced him to start moving and, as a result, he felt better about himself and about life. His new beginning contributed to his turning point. Then, of course, this turning point enabled him to have some more new beginnings.

But to have a true new beginning, you do need a turning point somewhere in the mix, whatever the order. Otherwise it looks new but it is same old, same old underneath. It can be almost instantaneous, as in Chad Varah's story, but it needs to happen. And, similarly, if you have a turning point it needs some kind of new beginning or it fades away or even hurts you.

Can you do without a catalyst?

No, you can't do completely without a catalyst, because something has to start you moving. But the catalyst can come from a time when you feel good enough that you fear you will be stuck there forever, as in Kate's story in Chapter 3 (see page 60), or for that matter from a lecture, a trip, a move or a significant birthday. In other words, you can start to make more out of less – more expansion out of less pain. Does this sound good?

CAN I STOP THERE?

Are you hoping you will be able to get through this difficult patch and then just settle back into a comfortable niche forever? This does sound tempting, but I'm afraid it doesn't really work like that.

You know in your heart that unless you are willing to confront challenges and renew yourself and your life periodically, you will stagnate or worse.

Change is always a risk. But not changing can be even riskier.

And, on another level, if life is not just about what you have or achieve, but also about what you are, this recurrent cycle of difficult times, turning points and new beginnings is part of becoming what you are or can be.

Chad Varah's biggest turning point was one in which he made a vow that led to an extraordinary new beginning. But it was certainly not his only one.

There was, for example, the time when he was still a young boy that his old Bishop told him some rudimentary facts about sex. In so doing, he set Chad Varah the example that enabled him to go on later to educate young children about sex without self-consciousness. There was also the time that the same Bishop convinced him to become a priest. Then there was the moment when Chad Varah realized that most of the telephone counselling that he did could be done by very simply trained people who were listening and befriending rather than counselling, and he set about creating an army of volunteers.

He considered each of these to be a turning point that contributed to who he was and what he gave to the world. He never stopped learning, and applying what he learned, to the groundbreaking work he was doing.

Think of this journey from difficult times to new beginnings as just one voyage of a ship that has stood the test of time, has been challenged regularly by the winds and the storms – and even sometimes the incompetence of the captain and of those that sail her – yet it does eventually get through to safe harbours, and then dares to go out again.

The ship is made for many voyages, many challenges, many discoveries. Some will be more successful than others, but all offer some kind of opportunity.

Do you really want to settle for finding a safe harbour and staying there forever?

Don't answer that when you are feeling miserable because you might be tempted to say *Yes,* and then you'd miss all the wonderful adventures in store for you!

Your Spiritual Gym

Exercise 1:

Where Am I and
Where Do I Want to Be?

Materials needed: Oil pastels/crayons, a pen, five sheets of paper, and a notebook or file where you can keep these records of your journey. This notebook or file can become your Imagework Diary.

1. At the top of each of the five pages, write these headings, one per page:

   ♦ Where am I?
   ♦ Where do I want to be?
   ♦ What's stopping me?
   ♦ What do I need to get past this?
   ♦ What is my true nature?

2. Now start with the first heading, choose a colour or colours, whichever colour feels right, and start to 'make marks' as artists call it. In other words, don't try to draw a picture, just let your fingers do the work and see what happens. If you are very good at drawing, you might want to use your non-dominant hand so that you can truly surrender. Don't look for meaning now, just be curious about what will emerge. *This is not a work of art, and you cannot get this wrong, or fail in any way.*

3. Keep drawing for 3–4 minutes, and then stop, and write a few words, again without forethought. Just put pen to paper and surprise yourself with what you write.

4. Do the same with each of the other four headings.

5. Now take a look at your drawings, and see what you notice. Show the drawings to your Imagework buddy, if you have one, or to an interested friend and see what they notice.

6. What have you learned? What surprised you? What felt like something you knew but hadn't told yourself? Write about this in your Imagework Diary.

CHAPTER 2

How Your Worst Enemy Can Be Your Best Friend

Now that you have a sense of the journey you are about to take, I'd like to introduce your secret weapon, the one that can turn your worst enemy into your best friend.

When you are facing difficult times of any kind, or just feeling stuck and knowing it is time for a change, you need all the good friends you can get – and, if possible, no worst enemies.

You want people around who will do all the things friends or advisers do at their best: Love you, show compassion if you're in trouble but also remind you just how strong and wonderful you are, gently help you to stop denying painful truths and to start being more honest with yourself, point out your options, remind you of what you love and what you are good at, encourage you to keep going, and just help in any way they can without trying to take over. You want people who will invite you to expand, to be the most you can be.

You certainly don't want people who criticize you, blame you, tell you it's all your fault, make you feel hopeless and powerless, say that you might as well give up now. People like this are really pushing you to contract, make yourself smaller and weaker and more powerless.

But which worst enemy can also be your best friend?

Your own imagination, of course.

Your inner imagery has an amazing power, and it can

work to support and guide you or to attack and hold you back; in fact, to do all those things that good friends do, but also the things worst enemies do.

So whether you've got friends or enemies around you in your life – or even when you feel utterly alone – you've always got your own imagination. Let's make sure it is your best friend.

That is what Imagework is all about.

THE POWER OF YOUR IMAGINATION

Your deepest attitudes are held in the form of images or metaphors[1] and your view of the future will similarly begin as a picture or story or image that you may never question and may not even be aware of. These images, which often originate in very early childhood, can guide your mind, your body, your emotions, and your most basic attitudes to life. Yet, you may never know this is happening.[2]

When does your imagination become your worst enemy? Whenever it attacks you, worries you, frightens you, humiliates you, blames you, criticizes you, or threatens you with some dire end you might come to – just like a bullying worst enemy might do.

For example, have you ever laid awake at night, terrified by what will happen to you if you get too old, too ill, too damaged by Alzheimer's, too poor, too lonely, too grief-stricken by the loss of a loved one, or all of the above? Or do you have some other haunting fear?

If you look closely you'll discover that your imagined picture of yourself should this or that happen is of you looking collapsed, small, young, helpless or hopeless. It is your image of yourself that is terrifying you more than the actual event. This is your imagination attacking you and getting you to contract, to stay safe, to go back into your cave.

Do you ever feel horribly humiliated as you remember a time in the past? Again, there's a memory picture of some kind in there, even if you can't see it right now, and it's so powerful that you are experiencing all those feelings all over again.

On the positive side, do you ever feel confident about the future? Do you have a picture or a sense of yourself feeling great, smiling happily and standing tall? This again is your imagination, being your friend, holding your hand, so that you feel safe even when things look risky from the outside.

Try this: *Let yourself have one of those fear or humiliation pictures, just for a moment, and see what happens to your body, your breathing, your heartbeat. Now see yourself happy, whether in the past or the present or the future. Step into that picture of you, and breathe into being this happy you. Now how does your body respond? What happens to your posture? To your breathing? To your mood? Are you smiling? Do you feel happier or lighter? Can you see how powerful these imagined memories can be?*

Your images can directly affect your autonomic nervous system, the one that includes your heart rate, digestion, respiratory rate, salivation, perspiration, that sort of thing, all of which we normally think of as beyond our control.[3]

◆

Try this: *Tell yourself to salivate. How well does it work? Now, vividly imagine sucking a very sour lemon. Does this work better?*

Neuroscientists have discovered that when you see or do something in your imagination, it activates many of the same parts of the brain as when you are literally seeing something or doing something.[4] Imagined physical exercise increases your strength and performance almost as much as actual exercise, and your heartbeat and breathing increase when you are doing it.[5] Yes, believe it or not, imagining doing an exercise without physically doing it can make you fitter!

◆

Try this: *Bend over, keeping your legs straight, and see how far down you can reach with the tips of your fingers. Now breathe three times very slowly, and think of something that makes you feel peaceful. Breathe three times slowly again, and think of something that brings a smile to your face. Breathe three times slowly again, and send the energy down to your feet. Now imagine that you are lying in the hot sun, on a beautiful lawn. Picture the scene, hear the birds, smell the freshly cut grass and feel the sun on your back. As the sun warms you, imagine that you find your body is getting softer* *and softer and more and more flexible. In fact, it is now made of some kind of magical rubber so that you can do anything you want to do. Imagine doing a forward then backwards somersault. Imagine rolling yourself up in a ball and then unroll yourself. Imagine reaching up and stretching to twice your height. Imagine seeing a high fence and jumping over it almost as if you are flying. Now your body can do anything you've ever wanted to do, explore more possibilities. When you are ready, come back to your physical body in the room. Now, bend over again. Can you reach any further than before? Or should I ask, how much further can you reach?*

In other words, your imagery is real and has real effects. It makes sense that everything you want to learn or do or achieve works better when you enlist the help of your imagination.

And for that matter, your imagination can help you solve most difficulties, for this is where the problems so often begin. I have found through my own research, for example, that the most effective way to deal with an extreme fear of the future is not the obvious one of increasing your level of financial and other security so that you can feel safer. Instead, you need to work with the images that are bringing that fear about. Once you've done that, you can calmly assess what positive actions you really need to take to protect yourself, something you cannot do in the grips of terror.

Think of it like being in the middle of a nightmare.

You can wake up in a panic and take a long time to calm yourself down, even though nothing is objectively happening in the room. If you want to vanquish the monster that has been chasing you, you must do it in your imagination, rather than by looking under the bed for a living, breathing monster.

Using imagery has been shown to deepen and speed up any learning, problem-solving or creative process. It is a central feature of methods from psychotherapy to business consultancy to sports psychology. Successful, highly skilled, healthy and creative people all use imagery naturally.[6]

In other words, your imagination is so central to your life that it's worth putting in a little effort to get it on your side.

WOULDN'T IT BE WONDERFUL?

Wouldn't it be great if all the images that are secretly guiding you could be clearly revealed to you? And wouldn't it be wonderful to know how to rid your mind of any images that have been blocking you in your life, and to create new ones that take you where you want to go?

Wouldn't it help to know a fast and easy way to gain access to your imagination, so that you can hear the whisperings of your heart and soul before they become shouts and get you into trouble? And to know that inner guidance is available from deep inside you to draw a map of the future that is in line with your highest purpose and your greatest joy?

And wouldn't it be comforting to have your images holding your hand every step of the way so that you never feel out of touch with your own inspiration and will?

You can and you will.

MARK'S STORY

My friend Mark, who is an internationally recognized management consultant, wrote me this story of how he started on his present life trajectory 21 years ago. It all began, apparently, when he did some visioning straight out of my book, *Life Choices, Life Changes*[7]. This was long before we met in person.

At the age of 31 I was faced with a frustrating (if well-paid) job in a large corporation. I was doing an MBA degree with the Open University at the time, and one of the tutors had recommended your book on 'Life Choices' as a possible route to think about what I might do next. So, one evening I lay on the bedroom floor in my small flat, relaxed and started to visualize... I saw a house with me in it... working upstairs... and other people, also involved in the work (I was single at the time)... and a garden... and a sign outside the door, a brass plate... and a way of life very different to the one I was living at the time.

After about 15 minutes, I got up from the floor. Life really was never the same again. I started working towards this new future right away – exploring setting up in business as a management consultant (which I did a year later), starting a relationship (a few months later), working with other people (pretty much right away)... and also starting to look for the house. It wasn't a case of 'the' house, but finding a place that would fit. The amazing thing was how quickly it all came together – and around 18 months after lying down on my bedroom floor, I was living in a house just like the one I had seen in my mind's eye.

And… 21 years on, I've moved twice, but always to a house with the same spirit, and carried on similar work… and I'm still with the same partner! And it's been an amazing journey, and at the same time things are still rather like they began on my bedroom floor in the little flat all those years ago. Strange, eh?

Mark's story is one of so very many that people have told me about over the years, where through visioning they sensed the right future for them and then went ahead to create or find it and enjoy it.

Was Mark predicting the future, or did he make it happen? I think it is a bit of both. The visioning taps into your best and deepest intuitive understanding of what is the path forward most in line with the person you are, and then, because you have a clear map and you know you are on track, you go ahead and make it happen relatively easily. When you are clear in this way, serendipitous events – or happy coincidences – seem to happen with amazing frequency to help you.

This is the magic and the mystery of visioning.

You will find a version of the visioning exercise Mark used on page 139.

DOROTHY'S STORY

Dorothy came to my Life Choices, Life Changes imagery workshop at our Atsitsa Centre on Skyros Island[8] 27 years ago, and reappeared in my Turning Points and New

Beginnings workshop in London just this year.[9] She told the group movingly about the extraordinary changes in her life that had ensued from that first workshop, and in particular from an imagery exercise I call Image as Life Metaphor, which involves inviting an image to emerge in response to a question and then working with it.

I asked participants to invite an image to emerge spontaneously that somehow represented who they were or what they needed to know at this moment in their lives. Dorothy's image was of a parrot in a cage. Interestingly enough, the image of an animal locked in a cage is a relatively common one when people do this exercise; in my experience, it always transpires that the cage door is open or the key is accessible. This is Dorothy's account:

You asked me to write about my Imagework experience at Atsitsa in 1986. I imagined I was a colourful parrot trapped in a cage and felt I was stuck. At the time I was stuck in my anorexia, very thin and somewhat physically frail. You helped me to find the key inside the cage and I let myself out, flapped my wings and ran around the circle. This work led directly to my starting to learn to fly a plane! Then, of course, I had to stay well for that, so I recovered from anorexia and then gave up my job as a lawyer and became a commercial pilot and flying instructor. Twenty-seven years on, I run a successful business training other people to become flying instructors and in many instances 'to live the dream'. Next year, I will be the first ever woman to become the Master of the Guild of Air Pilots and Air Navigators, after 85 years of existence, all due to the image of the parrot in the cage. I still try to be the parrot out of work, wearing colourful clothes and parrot earrings.

Dorothy's story is a wonderful reminder of how imagery can lead us from difficult times to a turning point in how we see the world and ourselves, and eventually to build our new understanding into a new beginning. In her case, the new beginning was this extraordinary and lasting change in her health, her career and her life.

You will find a version of the Imagework exercise Dorothy used on page 64.

PAST ITS SELL-BY DATE

Mark and Dorothy were consciously using imagery in a positive way to understand and guide their lives. When you are not working in this focused way, much of your existing imagery can be completely outdated, because it comes from vivid impressions and experiences you had when you were young or powerless. Sometimes the worst experiences are the ones you have completely forgotten, but your imagination has not, and the body tensions that go with those memories are still there under the surface, creating fear, anxiety or depression without your knowing why.[10]

For example, unconsciously you may have brought forward from your infancy an image of life as forever disappointing, or of people being aggressive and dangerous, or of good fortune being something that you have to pay for, or of every effort of yours being attacked, perhaps because in your childhood it was often that way. Of course, you may equally have unconsciously brought forward an image of a benevolent and abundant world, where there is always enough milk and always enough love and protection, and then your adult world will look very different!

One of my students, Catherine, was regularly sexually abused by her father when she was a child, but her father was also the one who mothered and seemed to love her, while her mother completely withdrew. In her mind, even nice guys can abuse you so how can you tell if a man is dangerous? So she closed down, put a *Do Not Enter* sign on her heart and never let herself get involved emotionally with a man. She had no idea she was doing it. She just wondered why she was always alone.

Now that Catherine is beginning to realize why and how she closed down, she's working to bring her old images up to date so that she can be open to a new relationship. She is learning that there is a way she can tell whether a man is dangerous. It's not by looking, because he may look like a nice guy. Rather it is by some other kind of intuitive sensing that tells her if this is a man with empathy, and if this is a man who respects women. Armed with this new awareness, she is preparing to open the door to relationships for the first time. She likes to imagine that there is a sensor on the door that will tell her whether the man is safe, so that she can decide whether to open the door to him and really let him in.

Now that Catherine knows that she is able to discriminate between men that are good for her and those that aren't, a new beginning is finally possible.

Like Catherine, you may not be fully aware that when

your adult life still looks like the world of your childhood, it can be because you have closed down to any new relationships or experiences that might counteract that view. Perhaps you have unconsciously been seeking out events that fit your picture, even managing to get people to behave in just these terrible ways. You may have been attracted to the kind of people who will behave this way, and ignored anyone who behaves well or considered them exceptions. What you see in the world is often what your inner eye has projected onto the world.

In other words, you see what you believe.

Does this begin to explain why sometimes, no matter how hard you try, you seem to end up in the same old situations you are trying to escape from?

AN EDUCATED IMAGINATION

The language of the imagination is the language of the child. And we all know that children can veer between being bullies and angels, sometimes with not much in between! So if we think of the imagination as a child, we can understand a bit better how to deal with it.

Let's take this a step further. If you adopt a child who has been treated badly, you'd have to take time to understand what has gone wrong, and to help the child get new attitudes. Similarly, if you have had a difficult childhood, your imagination will reflect that, and will need your loving attention.

On the other hand, if you adopt a child who has been treated well, you'd have less to deal with and a much easier ride. Similarly, those areas of your life that were happy and nourishing will have left a positive imprint on your imagination and will already be supporting you.

But any way you look at it, a child needs to be educated. Your imagination is the same – it needs education – and you are the teacher.

Think of it this way: Our formal education was all about words and numbers, because this is what helps us to understand, communicate with and manage the world. But our imagery, which helps us to understand, communicate with and manage ourselves, was never taught to us. So we need to educate ourselves as adults.

Your images of the future are crucial when you are setting out on a new path. If you are having a difficult time, your imagination may well be running riot, and probably torturing you with images of what you have lost, or where you went wrong, or what could go wrong in the future. Whatever plans you make will come out of this very painful mindset.

Even what you think you want will probably be based on old unconscious expectations or childhood images, so that you are likely to have a distorted picture of what you want now, as an adult, and what the future may hold. You may also have an old fear of defeat and failure, which will make it difficult for you to take the risk of going outside your comfort zone to have a genuine new beginning. After all, no risk comes with a cast-iron guarantee of success.

You may even be making predictions that no matter what you do, the way you are feeling now is how you will always feel, so you might as well give up.

Don't. Your imagination can become your best friend if only you pay it some attention, listen to it, and help it to help you, as Mark and Dorothy did.

Then, when you vision the future in a more creative way that taps into your inner wisdom, you may find that what would really bring you joy and purpose is very different to what you thought rationally is right for you.

Einstein once said: 'Imagination is more important than knowledge. For knowledge is limited to all we now know and understand, while imagination embraces the entire world, and all there ever will be to know and understand.'[11]

History repeats itself because your old thoughts and images push you that way. But it doesn't have to. Life is much richer than that, and so is your imagination. You really can have a new beginning.

Try this: 8 Tips to Harnessing Your Imagination
Here are some principles that will help you do your Spiritual Gym exercises, and indeed any imagery or visualization, easily and effectively. Please review these tips each time you do a Spiritual Gym exercise or any imagery or visualization exercise at all, until they become second nature.

1. *Never do this when driving a car or operating machinery, and do create a time and space where you won't be bothered by interruptions. It helps to start with some kind of relaxation. You can use any method you know that works for you, or try this one:*

   a. Breathe ten breaths, leaving a space after

*each outbreath and inbreath. Roll your
eyeballs up, hold them and let them drop.*

b. *Focus on your whole body and say, 'My whole
body, relax, deeply relax, completely relax.'
Now focus on each body part in turn and say;
'The crown of my head, relax, deeply relax,
completely relax' and so on through your body.
Notice, particularly, relaxing your eyelids,
letting your jaw drop and keeping it dropped,
relaxing your shoulders and spine. Then focus
on your mind: 'My mind, relax, deeply relax,
completely relax.' Then on your emotions: 'My
emotions, relax, deeply relax, completely relax.'*

c. *Now imagine you are bringing down a
big ball of light from above you, pulling
it through your body, and everywhere it
touches it relaxes, softens, brings peace, and
absorbs whatever doesn't benefit you. Finally,
let it roll through your heels into the earth,
depositing all that it has absorbed to be
transformed. Then invite a feeling of lightness
from the earth through your feet, your torso,
your neck and your head, and release it as if
through a hole in the top of your head.*

d. *Say to yourself, 'Now surrender.'*

2. *You need to engage your inner senses in order
to really connect with your imagination. At the
moment that you are experiencing something*

that is not there in the room with you, you are in the world of the imagination.

I use the word 'senses', which doesn't just mean visualizing or seeing. As I explained in the Introduction, you may not be visual, and I myself am not, which is why I call this Imagework and not Visualization. So if you're wondering what happens if you can't 'see' images, just trust me that this is not a problem. I can't, and yet my inner imagery is a central guiding factor in my life.

When I ask people to imagine a peach, feel its furry skin, smell it, turn on a rusty tap and wash it and listen to the squeak of the tap, and then taste it, everyone experiences this peach differently. Of course, no matter how well I describe that peach, each person will have a different peach in mind. But besides that, different senses will be stronger for different people.

Go ahead and imagine a peach in your hand. Can you see it as if it were there in the room with you? If so, you are very visual. If not, tell me the colour anyway! I'm sure if you let yourself, you will sense or see the colour even if you are not visual.

This does not mean you should just think about peaches and remember their usual colour. That is a thought, not an image, and it simply won't work. You need to be able to sense the peach as if it is there right now, not think of what it should look like.

When I imagine a peach, not being visual, I think of it like seeing 'through a glass darkly'. I don't so much see it as sense its presence, and I do sense and know the colour.

Similarly, can you feel it? Smell it? Hear the squeaky tap? Taste it? Sense its presence? Try it out and see which senses are strongest. As long as you have some sense of this peach, you are having an image, whether you see it, smell it, or sense it in any other way.

I remember the time I did some imaging with my students, and one of them met me in the cafeteria and told me I was some kind of witch. 'Why?' I asked. 'Because you created those people in the room.' At first, I just didn't know what she was talking about. 'Do you mean you really saw them as if they were in the room with you?' I finally asked. And yes, she did. Not being visual myself, it was the first time I realized how vividly many people could see images. Now when I do a workshop, I ask, 'How many of you can see this peach as if it were here in the room with you?' and the majority tend to raise their hands. Then I ask, 'How many cannot?' The remaining few raise their hands, and so do I.

3. *Let me emphasize again that this is not a test you can fail at. When doing imaging, it helps to imagine you are five years old and just playing at it. Images are natural, and are a child's first*

language. But if it feels like a task you might fail at, it becomes anxiety provoking, so you close down rather than expand, and cannot get in touch with the world of your free imagination. It's like trying to tickle yourself: The more you want it, the less it works. So go with whatever you get, no matter how vague, and run with it.

But don't decide you can't do it, and just 'think of something'. If it doesn't have the flavour of surprise about it, it is probably a thought and not an image. Let it go, and just open an empty space, and see what happens.

4. *Take the first image that comes to you, and if there is more than one, take the one that came first, and if more than one came almost simultaneously, take the one that feels most full of energy. Do not reject an image because it seems not to make sense or not to be very you or it seems negative or not good enough. The next image you get instead just won't work well. The images that are most difficult to accept are often the ones that have the biggest treasure locked up in them. Don't miss them.*

5. *It helps to record images in writing or in drawings. As with dreams, it is easy to forget the most profound experiences, and you want them to stay with you and enhance your life. This is why it is so good to have some colours – oil pastels or even crayons are perfect – and a file or workbook to use as your Imagework Diary, and*

to record your images in words and/or pictures. Sometimes, you can go straight to drawing, rather than starting with the image in your head, as in the Spiritual Gym exercise on page 27. Keep the diary and the colours available each time you do a Spiritual Gym exercise.

6. *If at all possible, do get a buddy who wants to do this with you, and with whom you feel safe to be yourself. This will help enormously to keep you on track, and also to enable you to surrender into a deeper level of your imagery.*

7. *If you've gone deep into relaxation, and are finding it hard to come back to normal waking consciousness, it is good to say to yourself at the end (or have your buddy say to you) 'I'm going to count up from 1-5 and when I say 5 I'm going to open my eyes (you're going to open your eyes), relaxed and alert, bringing the peace and wisdom back with me (with you). 1-2-eyelids lightening-3-4-coming to the surface-5. Eyes open. I stamp my feet (Stamp your feet) and come back to the room.' 3 stamps. Make sure you do this especially if you have to go into a difficult or challenging situation, or need to operate machinery.*

8. *Enjoy. And try to leave all the interpretations for later, once the whole exercise is finished. Then a good question to ask is 'Where in my life do I feel like this?'*

....

Your Spiritual Gym
Exercise 2:
Wise and Loving Being

....

Materials needed: Imagework Diary and oil pastels or crayons.

1. Use a relaxation technique. You can use any method you know or the one on page 42, or try this shorter one: Close your eyes. Roll your eyes up to the ceiling. Forget your eyes. Notice any tension in your body. Say hello to it and smile. Forget your body. Imagine a big light above your head, larger than your shoulders, and pull it slowly through your body, imagining that everywhere it touches, it relaxes, softens, heals, brings peace, and absorbs whatever doesn't benefit you. Finally it sinks through your feet into the earth, depositing whatever it has absorbed to be transformed. Allow a lightness to come up from the ground through your whole body, and then out through the top of your head. Surrender. Let go and see what happens.

2. Allow a memory to come up of a very difficult time you had in the past. See it, feel it, sense it. Open your heart for a moment to feel those emotions. Then float above and observe it, as if you were a wise and loving being floating above and watching over this person you were then and helping him or her. We'll call this person Past Self.

3. As the wise and loving being, ask yourself: What happened? What choices did Past Self make? Why? Was there an alternative? What did Past Self learn, if anything? If they did, how did that learning make a difference? Did they come through and how?

4. Send your love down to that Past Self who is struggling so, tell them that they are going to be okay, and appreciate them for bringing you where you are now. Come back to being Past Self, and receive that love and encouragement and insight.

5. Now picture the situation you are in now, and then float above it, and look at yourself as if from the perspective of the wise and loving being. We'll call the person you are now Present Self. What is happening now? What choices is Present Self making? Why? Is there an alternative? Is Present Self learning anything? What do you as a wise and loving being think Present Self needs in order to make this end happily, or at least to help them get through it? Whisper something to Present Self to help them on their way.

6. Send your love and support and a dollop of what Present Self needs, and then float down into the situation, step back into being Present Self, and receive this love and support.

7. Now ask yourself this question about both events: Supposing I believed that I chose these events, what did I choose them for? (Forget that you may not believe the

situation is anything more than chance or fate, and don't conclude that I think it was good for you and 'meant to be'. Just challenge yourself to answer the question hypothetically.) Now ask yourself: Would I choose it again? Be open to whatever answer comes.

I asked this question of a client of mine who had been a top young athlete and dancer, and who now has MS. After realizing that her physical freedom and success had hidden costs (such as always being an outsider and envied) and that her present limitations have hidden bonuses (such as a tremendous push forward in other areas of her development, and an understanding that nothing physical can stop her), she said to her own surprise, 'I would choose both again. But now, I've learned what I had to learn and I need to get better soon. I'm going to do whatever I can to get my health back.' And she made a promise to herself to go back onto the health regime she had abandoned.

8. Now record your experience in your Imagework Diary, with words, drawings or whatever speaks to you. What do you notice? Use this record later to remind you of where you have been and what you have learned. Don't let it fade away as your dreams so often do. The more vivid you keep your experiences, and the more attention you pay to recording them, the more they can go on working for you.

9. If you are still feeling a bit in a trance, count yourself up or have your buddy count you up: 'I'm going to count up from 1–5 and when I say 5 I'm going to open my eyes (you're going to open your eyes), relaxed and alert, bringing the peace and wisdom back with me (with you). 1-2-eyelids lightening, 3-4-coming to the surface, 5. Eyes open. I stamp my feet (stamp your feet) and come back to the room.' Three stamps.

CHAPTER 3

Difficult Times
Make Change Easy

Writer Sue Townsend, whose burnout story featured in my book The Joy of Burnout,1 is no stranger to difficult times. She once remarked to me that when people feel that something has gone seriously wrong and changed or disrupted their life, they often say, 'I can't wait to get back to my life.'

'Don't they realize,' she said, 'that this is their life?'

Difficult times do not happen once or twice in a lifetime. They are a normal part of a fulfilling and creative life, of your life.

But if you are having a difficult time don't just get stuck in a head-in-the-sand approach, refusing to read the writing on the wall. When your world changes within you or around you, you need a new way of seeing, and indeed of being. This is particularly urgent when the changes are painful ones. And since neither you nor your life ever stops changing, you will need to keep finding new and more expanded ways of seeing and being.

If the time is right, and if you are willing, then life changes and challenges, no matter how difficult, can become turning points that lead to new beginnings.

CHRIS'S STORY

Chris is my neighbour in Hastings, where I live part-time. She moved to Hastings from Yorkshire after her husband died. I asked her to tell me the story of the journey she must have taken from bereavement to new beginnings. This is the story she told me:

Two years ago, she lost her husband of 33 years. It was a happy marriage, and they used to do everything they could together. When he died, she was devastated. Her cigarette smoking immediately went up from 20 to 50.

But slowly she began to accept the fact that her life would never be the same nor would her plans for the future. She stopped the struggle, acknowledged her difficult feelings and faced her new reality. Eventually, she accepted that she was still here, still alive and kicking, and that she needed to move on. She also realized that some things were possible now that hadn't been while her husband was alive.

She'd never liked Yorkshire, but he had, so they had stayed there. She didn't want to live in a big house and couldn't manage the garden because of her arthritis, but he did, so they had stayed there. As much as she loved him, now that he was gone, she was free to follow her own tastes in life. And she decided to do just that.

She wanted to live by the sea, so she took out a map and stuck a pin in the small seaside town of Hastings, which she had vaguely heard of. She decided to go there, even though she'd never been before and knew no one.

This whole process was her turning point. Next came the new beginning – putting her realizations into practice.

Serendipitous events, or happy coincidences, often occur when we are working with our intuition or putting our visions into practice. For Chris, these came in the form of people who helped her. A man from the war pensions department visited her out of the blue, told her she should be due a pension on account of her husband's veteran status, and helped her to apply for it. When his own department vetoed it, he encouraged her to appeal and even helped her fill out all the forms. She won the case and this gave her the financial security to follow her heart.

To the background chorus of her friends saying she was crazy, she quit her job, sold her house and came down to Hastings, staying in a hotel until she found a place to rent. It was a mark of her newfound freedom that, against rhyme or reason, she could surrender to the intuition that told her where to make her new life. She found another helpful stranger in Hastings, the clerk at the hotel she stayed in when she was looking for a flat. He suggested to her where in Hastings he thought she'd be happy, and then looked with her on the internet for vacancies. They found a flat there for rent at that very moment. She saw the flat, loved it, took it immediately and that is how she became my neighbour. Now she knows everyone around, has her daughter living not far away, and lives in the presence of the sea, which she loves. She is at home in her own skin, and values her solitude as well as her neighbourliness.

I have worked with quite a few women over the years who told me that when their beloved husband died, they suddenly went ahead to get educated, start a career or express themselves in some other way. It didn't mean that they weren't in great pain when their husband died, only that they took the opportunity life gave them along with the grief and ran with it.

WHY DIFFICULT TIMES ARE CATALYSTS

Nobody really wants difficult times that they haven't consciously chosen. While some people challenge themselves purposely with activities such as mountain climbing where anything that happens is part of the adventure, unexpected disasters and losses and illnesses are seldom welcomed.

The good news is that even the worst events can bring their own rewards. Many people never get started on turning points and new beginnings if they haven't been pushed by some kind of difficult time. This is why serious illness is so often called 'a wake-up call', and why people so commonly say that they are grateful for their illness, no matter how awful it was or is by any objective standard.

There are times in life when you must simply stay on course, and when persistence is your greatest virtue. But there are also times when you know the winds of change are blowing, and you need to listen. Yet the power of inertia coupled with the fear of failure can be very compelling. It's hard to leave a warm snug bed when the world is looking cold and a bit scary.

After all, getting going is a big deal, and you might fail and better the devil you know. As long as you are relatively comfortable, why not stick with the familiar and at least you'll have a reasonable time?

Or so you believe.

The trouble is that if the familiar is already not all that great, sticking with it seldom gives you the security and peace of mind you expect. This is because of that phenomenon commonly known as the slippery slope. I've taken thousands of people through imagery exercises about life change. In one of the exercises I do, which I will show you in Chapter 7 (see page 139), people imagine travelling to a positive future, one in which they are truly honouring themselves, and to a negative one, in which they feel miserable because they are abandoning, betraying or trapping themselves. Then they look back and see how they got to these very different futures. (This is actually the exercise that Mark did in Chapter 2 – see page 35).

It turns out that getting to the miserable future was easy. They just kept on doing what they were doing. To get to the positive future, on the other hand, they had to up their game, refocus, change an attitude, do something new.

In other words, staying on a not very good path and just keeping on doing what you are doing may well turn out to be the slippery slope to a reality that is pretty awful.

Fortunately or unfortunately, life seldom lets you stand still forever even if you try to. If you are reading this book, it's probably because you've realized that staying where you are isn't really going to work. You have already started moving, though perhaps not in a direction you are happy about. Now you have to make some choices.

YOUR DECISIONS ARE MORE IMPORTANT THAN YOU THINK

People in a crisis are more open than at any other time to taking advice, to making fundamental shifts. This may be because the question during a difficult time, or a crisis, is no longer 'Will I move?' but 'Which way will I move?' And the decisions you make are very crucial, because they determine not only your future life, but also your future character. Each important choice you make at these times makes it more likely that you will make a similar choice in future.[2]

There are two basic ways you can respond:

You can try to stand still, which in effect means going backwards. Think of trying to stay in the same place on a moving escalator.

Or you can go forward to meet whatever is coming towards you.

Contract or expand.

Give up on life or accept and move on.

The first way standing still, contracting, giving up is a recipe for more trouble than you are in already. The second is an opening towards a turning point and a new beginning.

Times of crisis or change demand that you step forward into a bigger picture of who you are and where you are going. If you do, you will be able to respond positively to whatever has happened, and make clear and effective choices. Each positive choice also makes it easier for you to be flexible and creative in the future.

As you get into the habit of consistently choosing openness rather than stuckness, your whole neural pattern and personality changes, and you find your life is evolving in line with your deepest values and in the direction of joy.

If instead you retreat and go backward instead of forward, you may contract with fear and stress and start having other problems, including health issues. You will also be more likely to make a similar choice next time.

You will miss the opportunity that life, and your own heart and soul, have offered you.

Since difficult times are going to get you moving one way or another, for better or for worse, why not go for better? It is better not just for you, but for everyone around you and for all the more far-flung people who would benefit from your shift. What is in your highest best interest is in the highest best interest of everyone around.

What would have happened if Chad Varah (see page 16) had just gone home, got depressed at the state of the world and felt helpless to do anything instead of making the vow that led him to help so many people?

His choices mattered and so do yours.

You matter, and you make a difference.

ARE YOU BEING PUSHED OUT OF YOUR COMFORT ZONE? There are three basic kinds of difficult times that are catalysts for new beginnings: The ones that push you out of your comfort zone, the ones that pull you forward with a promise or a possibility for the future, and those that are symptoms of an overdue or missed turning point or new beginning.

Let us start with the difficult times that push you out of your comfort zone and into an uncomfortable or painful place. You might have lost someone or something important to you. You might have become ill, unemployed or bereaved. You might feel betrayed, abandoned or abused by someone you trusted personally or professionally. You might have been shocked or disillusioned by something happening in the world around you.

Such events are, as you know when you are in touch with your wisest self, normal parts of life. But this seldom helps when you are right in the middle of all the feelings. You may never have thought it could happen to you, that your life could be shattered in this way, and you may be feeling lost, abandoned or unutterably heartbroken.

Sometimes, what has changed is not to do with events or people in your life, but rather with your own attitudes to your life. What felt good no longer feels good. It may have fit the person you were but not the person you are now and want to become. You have already moved on.

This too is normal. We are not meant to stay in the same place forever. Where would the learning and the challenge and the expansion and the new growth be?

Whatever has pushed you out of your comfort zone, something inside or outside is whispering: *The old way has come to an end. A new way is beckoning.*

ARE YOU BEING PULLED BY THE FUTURE?

Sometimes nothing has changed yet, inside or outside, but you know it can or will.

In other words, difficult times are not always what we would conventionally call painful periods in life. They may be times that you find difficult because you know you have to move on and you find this hard.

Perhaps what has held you committed to your present situation no longer does, and as the old bonds are released you become aware of what it is you want to move on to. Perhaps the future is actively beckoning you with a new job, a new relationship, a new home. Yet if your present situation is not too bad, you may find it easier to stay put than to rouse yourself and get going.

This is what happened to my friend Kate, a psychotherapist and jazz singer. Here is her story:

> A friend of mine came to look at my garden, and said I needed to bring down the Leylandii trees. I was so reluctant to do it that she said, 'The trouble with you is that you want the change without having to go through the process of the change.' She was so right, not just about my garden, but about my whole life.
>
> I was ready for change. I had lived in my house for 25 years, my son had moved away happily, I had bought out my ex-partner so I was no longer in a relationship with him, and my mother who lived nearby was moving to an old people's flat. The ties were being cut.
>
> Then when I was teaching my course in Skyros, someone quoted their coaching guru as saying, 'Take massive decisive action.' I thought, 'If I am not going to lie in bed, looking at that light on the ceiling, feeling okay, but knowing I'm going to die in this bed, I'm going to have to do it.'
>
> Within a year, I moved to London, and started the relationship with my present partner. The difficulty was that that I could have stayed in my old situation forever.

Change is always challenging, and can easily feel threatening, even when it is offering something good. Getting married and moving house are usually considered positive choices, yet they are very high on the list of stressful life events.

Sometimes, your fear of the future is activated when you step into the unknown. If you're moving to a new home, you may picture yourself as being lonely, depressed, out of place and wishing you'd stayed put. This is not going to make that move easy!

Though the scenario is different, the message is still the same: *The old way has come to an end. A new way is beckoning.*

HAS A MISSED TURNING POINT OR NEW BEGINNING COME BACK TO HAUNT YOU?

Burnout, a subject I know a great deal about both from my own experience and from my research, is a good example of a problem that results from an overdue turning point or new beginning.

My own burnout stopped me in my tracks, and I didn't regain my full energy for years. But at the time, I didn't know what had hit me, didn't even recognize that it was a classic case of burnout. Much later I realized that I had had my turning point vision but I had been unable to go onto a new beginning.

The burnout was the result of that very failure to follow through.

I had seen clearly that it was time for me to go inward, let go of the stress of my over-busy life for a while and reach a new sense of myself. But my outdated images of being a 'good girl' who wasn't selfish had taken over and instead of going inward, I helped my then husband start a new magazine. Because I was divided against myself, I started to drive myself forward.

I drove myself straight to burnout. Once I was burnt out, I knew I had no choice but to stop and listen, and to turn that turning point into a real new beginning.

Some people don't do this even after they've burnt out. They are determined to get better so they can go back to the same situation that caused the burnout.

Are you suffering from a missed turning point or new beginning?

Perhaps, like me, your heart went out of something but you did it anyway and, what's more, you drove yourself forward relentlessly towards burnout or other illnesses and problems. Relationship failures, depression, panic attacks and many other difficulties can result from overdue turning points, from times that you knew in your heart of hearts that there was a challenge, risk or a step forward that was right for you but you didn't dare do it, or found reasons why it couldn't be done.

As I write this, I am reminded of a conversation I had many years ago with my father. My father was an eternal student, endlessly curious and ready to learn, and he was an early pioneer in the world of adult education and personal development. He went excitedly to the first personal development groups; in fact, it was he who introduced me to the personal development groupwork that was emerging in the sixties, which soon became central to my life and work.

I always smile when I remember how he used to complain that because he was usually the oldest one there, everyone asked him to role-play their fathers and grandfathers. He, of course, was just feeling like a little boy.

Some time after my mother died, he told me, 'I never

had the courage to ask her to come with me to one of these groups.' It made his heart sore, because the relationship and their life had gotten so stuck and dead.

He himself got out of his depressed world after her death, but he would have so loved to have taken her with him, or at least given her a chance for her own freedom. This was his deep regret. He promised himself he would be more courageous in future.

The message here? *The old way has* really *come to an end. Don't fudge it this time. It's time for the new way to begin.*

Now what?

Difficult times are not the end of the world, even when they feel like it. They are just the end of that particular world, or world-view, or life path, and the beginning of a new one. Indeed, they already contain within them the seeds of that new path.

I was talking to my son Ari once about a difficult time I was having, and he said, 'Mum, it's not the end of the world.' I said, 'But Ari, what is the end of the world?' He looked at me and smiled: 'The end of the world.'

So if you are reading this book, it is clearly not the end of the world, and therefore there is a way forward. Let's find it.

The first step is to say *Yes* to the journey ahead. Are you willing? If so, the journey has already begun. You have taken your first step.

Your Spiritual Gym
Exercise 3:
Image as Life Metaphor

Materials needed: Imagework Diary and oil pastels or crayons.

When you are in the middle of a difficult time, it helps to get a sense of what is going on under the surface, where you are stuck, if you are, and what it would take for you to move forward. This wonderful exercise will help you do just that. It helps you to diagnose on a deep and yet simple level your situation and your next step. You will find Dorothy's story about the profound effect of this exercise on her life on page 36.

The exercise involves inviting an image to emerge in response to a question and then working with the image that comes up. These images have the powerful ability to summarize the basic structure of whatever it is you are asking about. The background assumptions come to the foreground, the complexities become streamlined, the history of the situation becomes obvious, and a resolution can emerge where it seemed impossible before.

If you are doing this exercise on your own, you may have to keep looking at the page, and many people do it this way successfully. But it does help to have an Imagework buddy so you can read it to each other. Better still, you yourself, or both of you, can be guided through it by me if you download the MP3 from my website. (For books, CDs and MP3s see http://www.dinaglouberman.com/shop/).

Don't forget to review the *8 Tips to Harnessing Your Imagination* on page 42 before you start.

1. Relaxation. Use any method you know or try this from Chapter 2. If it is too long, just use any step or combination of steps that really works for you:

   a. Take ten slow breaths, leaving a space after each outbreath and inbreath. Roll your eyeballs up, hold them and let them drop

   b. Focus on your whole body and say, 'My whole body, relax, deeply relax, completely relax.' Now focus on each body part in turn and say, 'The crown of my head, relax, deeply relax, completely relax' and so on through your body. Notice particularly relaxing your eyelids, letting your jaw drop and keeping it dropped, relaxing your shoulders and your spine. Then focus on your mind: 'My mind, relax, deeply relax, completely relax.' Then on your emotions: 'My emotions, relax, deeply relax, completely relax.'

   c. Now imagine you are bringing down a big ball of light from above you pulling it through your body, and everywhere it touches it relaxes, softens, brings peace, and absorbs whatever doesn't benefit you, finally rolling through your heels into the earth, depositing it all into the earth to be transformed. Then invite a feeling of lightness from the earth through your feet, your torso, your neck and your head, and release it as if through a hole in the top of your head.

d. Say to yourself, 'Now surrender.'

2. Invite the image: Say to yourself, 'I'd like to allow an image to emerge of an animal, a plant or an object that somehow represents who I am or what I need to know at this moment in my life.' Now just relax and wait to see what comes up. It can come as a word, or a picture, or an impression or in any other way. As long as you have a feeling you know what it is, go with it.

3. Study the image: Observe the image and its environment from the sides, from above (an aerial view) and from underneath. What do you notice? How does the image relate to its environment?

4. Become the image: Step into the image and breathe into being the image. Ask yourself, 'What is the essence of being me right now? What is going on for me? What's the best of this? What's the worst of it? What do I love and what do I fear? How do I relate to my environment?'

5. Now ask yourself, 'What led up to this? Has it always been this way for me? Was there a time when things were different, or when I was different? If so, when did it all change and how? How did it used to be? Which do I like better?'

6. The soul's point of view: Imagine there is a large light outside the whole scene, larger than life itself. Become the light, and expand as light. Look at the image being and situation in your light and see what you notice. What can you see about the image being that it doesn't know about itself? What can you whisper to the image being to help it on its way? Then heal them with light, love, sound, hands, etc. How do they change? Now come back to yourself as the image being and receive those insights and that healing.

7. Ask yourself, 'What is possible? What's next? What's the way forward?' Whatever it is, do it and enjoy it.

8. Now ask yourself, 'If I could wave a magic wand over the situation, what would the perfect life be for me as the image being?' Let a picture come to mind, and experience it fully.

9. Appreciate and reflect: Appreciate yourself for your image, and reflect on what it means. What is one thing you learned from this, perhaps something you could say you knew but hadn't told yourself? Where in your life do you feel like this?

10. Drawing: Take paper and colours, and just let yourself express the image or the whole experience, without trying to control it in any way. Then write a few words, also completely spontaneously. What do you notice? Share it with your buddy if you are working with one and ask what they notice.

11. Looking forward: If this experience (not just the picture but the whole imagery experience) is a map of one aspect of your life, what is one thing you could do differently? You can try doing this exercise regularly, particularly if you feel you are on a bit of a roller coaster with your feelings, or you are just feeling stuck and don't know what is really bothering you or what to do about it.

12. If you are still feeling a bit in a trance, count yourself up or have your buddy count you up: 'I'm going to count up from 1–5 and when I say 5 I'm going to open my eyes (you're going to open your eyes), relaxed and alert, bringing the peace and wisdom back with me (with you). 1–2–eyelids lightening, 3–4–coming to the surface, 5. Eyes open. I stamp my feet (stamp your feet) and come back to the room.' Three stamps.

Variation: If you want to solve a particular problem, change the wording when you invite the image to 'I'd like to allow an image to emerge that somehow represents my work, or my relationship, or this particular problem and my relationship to it at this moment in my life.'

STEP TWO:

YOUR TURNING POINT

CHAPTER 4

Stop, Give up Hope and Keep the Faith

Of all the quite prominent people I interviewed for my series of articles about turning points in their lives, not one said that becoming successful or well known was their major turning point.

Rather, they all talked of a time when the penny dropped and a new understanding, a new relationship to life, emerged, usually through a difficult time. It seemed that they all took for granted that their turning point was an inner transformation, and that everything else followed.

Turning points are the subject of the next four chapters. A turning point is always an inner shift rather than an outer one. It is about going to a deeper level of yourself, looking at some of the attitudes that may be causing you distress and keeping you stuck, contracted, even moving backward, and then finding new attitudes that will help you find peace and a new way forward and a vision for where you are going.

Like turning the corner in a car, you need to slow down, not hurtle round at top speed.

I call this 'radical healing'. It's not about trying to get the old show back on the road, but about moving towards a new sense of who you are and who you can be. It's not a cure or a solution, but a resolution – a sense of peace and openness to the future.

Turning points have four aspects:

1. Surrendering to the present reality of your life.

2. Finding the part of you that is still there even if all hell has broken loose.

3. Opening up to an expanded picture of who you are and where you are going from here.

4. Visioning your future life or work.

Turning points need not happen in this order, and sometimes they all succeed each other in a moment, as in Chad Varah's story (see page 16).

This chapter is about the first aspect: Surrendering to what is, has been and will be. You unstick yourself not by beginning to move, but by opening your heart to where you are. Indeed, unless you stop pushing yourself and really honour who and what you are and what life has brought you at this very moment, no matter how painful, it is very difficult to have a true new beginning.

I like to put it this way: *Stop, give up hope and keep the faith.* This may sound counter-intuitive but please do read on. I want to start with two stories, one about my father, and one about my friend Loraine, both of whom had to stop, give up hope and keep the faith.

MY FATHER ISAAC'S STORY

This story is a rather unusual one, in that it is about a person who had just died. Please feel free to interpret it however you like – at face value, or as an image, dream or metaphor. For me, it was all literally true, though it did not take place in what is conventionally called 'the real world'.

My father, whom I mentioned briefly in Chapter 3, died rather suddenly while he was having an emergency operation in a New York hospital. As I live in London, I didn't get a chance to say goodbye in the normal sense of the word.

Yet we were so connected that as I tried to send him healing, I sensed the change at the moment of his death. I know this was really true, because I said to my husband, 'Either he has healed or he has died,' and I phoned the hospital immediately. The surgeon came to the phone sounding upset and told me that my father had just died on the operating table.

On the plane to the States just after his death, I had a series of images that seemed to be showing me what was happening to him after his death. It is hard to describe, except to say that it was as if I was tuning into a live video of something happening somewhere else. When I turned to do something else the images disappeared, but they continued when I closed my eyes again. I tried to stay focused because when I missed a bit, I just missed it; the story had continued. It all feels as vivid as if it were yesterday, though it happened almost 25 years ago.

I saw my father walking alone on his pathway, which I sensed to be his path of transformation from life to death, and then he began trudging up a hill with a big, heavy sack on his back. He paused for a moment, put the sack down and then picked it up again, as if he couldn't let go of it. Eventually he stopped, and started to empty out the sack. It transpired that it was full of the memories and feelings that tied him to life. This didn't include the love and positive memories, which left him free, but just the resentments and bitterness and 'if only' feelings.

Until that moment, I had no idea how many of these he was carrying, because he so seldom complained, nor had I quite understood how deeply damaging they were.

He sifted through them, and it seemed that his job was to look at each and then say, 'So be it' and let it go. This he did, one by one.

Once he had done that, and the sack was empty, he put it down and continued on his way. He started walking towards the light. Four angels came to greet him and began to massage him with light and love. I was so moved because latterly in his life, he was probably never massaged or even physically touched very much.

Always a modest man, he was marvelling at it all, and seemed to be saying, 'This feels like heaven. Why are they doing this for me?' I laughed and whispered, 'This *is* heaven.'

I said goodbye, and I left him surrounded by his angels. The images disappeared, never to return, but also never to be forgotten. *So be it* is one of my most helpful mantras and is at the heart of what is involved in stopping, giving up hope and keeping the faith.

Loraine's story

My friend Loraine told me how she discovered that her sister had done her out of her inheritance. Her mother had collected wonderful works of art worth millions, including even Ming Dynasty porcelain, and had intended these for her three children. But her sister had sold all the valuable pieces secretly, including ones her mother had held dear. Loraine felt murderous rage about having lost the financial security she had always wanted, and tremendous grief about her mother's wishes being betrayed.

I always feared being poor in old age, and all the while I had my future assured. By the time I found out how valuable my mother's art collection was, my sister had already sold it. My mother's friend told me that my mother used to say that just one of those porcelains could buy her a house.

The turning point came when I realized that if I carried out revenge as I wanted to, and could easily do, I'd get it back karmically. I am still angry but I feel there is an order, and you can't get away with things. It's an awareness that what goes around comes around, and if I just let the injustices go, justice sorts itself out, while if I retaliate, then it's going to come back to me.

Also, I had a memory that my sister felt I hadn't been there for her when she was 17 and pregnant. She asked me if I'd leave my family, with whom I'd just been reunited, and go with her to the countryside, but I didn't want to go. Then also my sister has had a real tragedy in her life; her son had cancer and he's still not out of the woods, and that made me realize what really matters. I also came to see that taking revenge would perpetuate the endless cycle of violence in the world.

What's come out of it is that I'm now about to take a course on conflict resolution and reconciliation, and hopefully this will keep me on the journey. I've been given this for a reason, and I've consciously decided to give it a meaning, which is that if I do believe in all this spiritual stuff, it makes sense on that level and this is my teacher.

STOP

Both my father and Loraine had to stop, give up hope of ever having what they had lost or been denied or been deprived of, and yet keep the faith that they were still okay.

So how do *you* stop, give up hope and keep the faith?

Just start by stopping!

When you are going through difficult times, you are likely to be in a battle with yourself or with life, or in a state of resignation, or a deep hopelessness. Something is wrong, and that is not all right. This was not on the menu, or at least it was not what you ordered. This is wrong, unfair, can't be happening to me, shouldn't be happening at all!

If at the same time you are doing everything you can to keep going, you may well be closing down, becoming tense and over-controlled, putting your mind in charge of your heart. Chris, who I talked about in Chapter 3, used cigarette smoking as an attempt to control her feelings. My father carried his resentments everywhere on his back, so as not to let go of them. And Loraine's desire for revenge was her way of gaining control over the situation, because it felt too painful to simply open her heart and experience all those terrible feelings.

So the first step is to stop the struggle, and simply feel your feelings, without judging them as bad or wrong with what I call your 'control mind'. Your 'control mind' is the bit of your mind that tries to keep everything safe, predictable and under control. You can recognize it because generally the thoughts feel as if they are in your forehead, rather than emerging from your body, heart or soul.

You may find it difficult to separate out the feelings in your heart and body from your thoughts in your 'control mind'. These thoughts can include your predictions of how things will be in future, your judgements of whether the feelings are good or bad, your attempts to tell yourself you are being silly or should pull yourself up by your bootstraps, your regrets for the mistakes you believe have brought you here, your decision to get back at those who have harmed you and teach them a lesson, indeed any conclusions about the past, present and future.

Even when the events that are happening are generally considered positive ones – a new job, a marriage or the birth of a baby, perhaps – you may be having a tough time emotionally. You may be berating yourself because you have negative feelings you think you shouldn't have, or are simply not enjoying these experiences as much as you think you should.

All these judgements are methods that your mind can use to control the 'irrational' feelings. Yet these feelings are perfectly sensible when honoured.

It helps to notice the thoughts, and find out where they are in your body. Are they in your forehead area? If so, they probably come from your 'control mind'. Try going into your heart to listen to what it is feeling, and into your body to sense what you are feeling. This will give you a much better idea of what you are really feeling.

Feelings are not predictions. Feelings are not judgements. Feelings in themselves are not dangerous. In fact, the feelings keep you human. They tell you what is going on for you, and whether it feels good or bad. They are information, and they are natural.

I'd like to emphasize that it's not that your mind is bad; it's simply that the role of your mind needs to change. Instead of using it to control or stop the pain or difficulty, it needs to expand and become a loving, wise witness or friend or parent that holds you in your pain and somehow assures you that you are okay.

You can learn also to be open to a larger mind, or wisdom mind, which offers you the intuitive knowledge that is really of service to you. Working with imagery in the way I am suggesting in this book will help you to do this on a regular basis.

That said, I can almost guarantee that many of these thoughts, judgements and predictions will plague you to a greater or lesser extent. The secret is to refuse to feed them. You feed them by believing in them or drawing conclusions from them, or arguing with them, or paying them any serious attention. Instead, you need to learn to let them drop out naturally.

In other words, know that you can't believe the thoughts in your 'control mind', and as soon as you become aware of them, switch channels in your mind, and distract yourself, or go for a walk, or have a cup of tea, or do whatever works for you.

If they come in the middle of the night, sit up immediately

and let the thoughts go. When you are lying down, it is easy for the thoughts to take over. If sitting up doesn't work, get out of bed, and do something distracting until they pass. Don't even try to fight the thoughts, because that feeds them. Just move on.

You might find a little mantra that works for you; for example, when I get into regrets, I tell myself, *This is it; there is no other* and that seems to shut up my control mind.

This is also where my father's *So be it* can come in handy. I like to say *So be it and I come back to centre*. The *So be it* refers not only to the facts, but also to the feelings about the facts, however unreasonable I think those feelings are. I acknowledge them, and then I do my best to come back to my grounded sense of self at my centre. In a sense, that is what Loraine is doing. She recognizes that she's been done a wrong, she accepts her rage, grief and desire for revenge, and yet she is trying her best to learn from it and come back to her centre, indeed to let it show her a new way forward.

Above all, stopping means keeping your thoughts, feelings and actions resolutely on the present situation. You do whatever you need to keep life going and to be present and loving to yourself and to others. But thoughts about the future, or what-ifs, are strictly forbidden until you've got through the feelings and found some resolution. Otherwise your plans will be tainted by the uncomfortable feelings you are having right now.

I like to think of this stopping as the *Shabbat* principle. In the Jewish tradition, on the Sabbath or *Shabbat* you only do what is necessary for that day, or what is inspiring, but not what needs to be accomplished for the future.

There is an old saying that 'It's not so much that Jewish

people kept the *Shabbat* but that the *Shabbat* kept the Jewish people.' The *Shabbat* principle has kept me safe at times when my mind was stressed and running riot, or my heart was full of pain. Indeed it has done the same for the many people I have worked with who were burning out or burnt out. It can do the same for you.

When I was growing up in New York, there was a famous advertisement for Levy's rye bread: *You don't have to be Jewish to eat Levy's.*

The same goes for the Shabbat.

VULNERABILITY AND NEEDINESS

One of the problems with stopping, letting yourself be vulnerable and feeling your feelings can be a fear of being needy. You probably don't like feeling needy, being seen as needy, or any variation thereof.

However needy and vulnerable are very different indeed.

When you are needy, you are feeling bad, but also expecting something from the outside world. *You should… If you loved me you would… Why doesn't anyone care more?* That sort of thing. That is not stopping and letting go of control; rather that is trying to take control by complaining that someone has failed you, or that you deserve something, or that you don't deserve this, or that life is betraying you, or whatever. You expect someone to fix it, and if no one does they are bad or you are unloveable.

Needy is controlling.

When you are vulnerable, on the other hand, you are simply stopping and feeling your feelings and honouring their importance to you. You are not implying that anyone, including yourself, should do something to fix it. Your feelings are there, for others to see, if you trust them. That's it. That's your reality and you are surrendering to it.

Vulnerable is surrendering.

Can you let yourself be vulnerable without expecting it to be fixed? Do you know that old saying, *If it ain't broke, don't fix it*? You're not broken. You're just sad, angry, hurt or feeling something else that is painful. That's the nature of reality – sometimes we hurt. Nothing is broken and no one is to blame and there's nothing to fix.

Remember this: You haven't done anything wrong, you're not wrong or bad to be where you are, and there is a way forward.

You don't need to know what that way forward is right now. You will, when the time is right.

GIVE UP HOPE

This idea that you must give up hope probably goes against everything you've ever heard. But it is not what it sounds like. It is not about hopelessness; rather it is the opposite of hopelessness. Let me explain.

The hope I am talking about is hope for something particular you believe you have to have to be okay. When you are facing or fearing loss or failure, look closely at what underlies the loss or failure. Often it is about losing some view of yourself or of your life that you hold dear.

When I interviewed people about burnout, it was the fear of losing some identity they considered core that drove them to keep going on a path they knew wasn't right for them. Similarly, when I interviewed people about their worst fears of the future, it turned out that what they feared was not the terrible event, but the fact that they believed that if they lost their health, livelihood, partner, sanity, mind or whatever, they would never be okay again.

Any hope for something we feel we can't do without is always accompanied by a fear that it won't happen or that we will lose it. This is why the Buddhist view is that 'attachment is suffering'. Attachment in this sense means an investment in something we consider essential to our survival, but is not.

To heal and move on from difficult times, therefore, you need to give up any hopes for whatever it is you believe your psychological survival depends on, and keep the faith that you will still be okay.

This is what my father was doing so poignantly when he was able to say, *So be it* about the painful memories of being denied things that he thought he needed, and thereby letting go of his resentments and suffering. This is also what Loraine is trying to do, by giving up on the lost financial security her mother intended her to have.

You need to give up hope not only of a better now, but also of a better past and a better future, if by better you mean something specific in the world that makes everything okay. To put it another way, you need to say *Yes* to reality. This is much harder than it sounds and it is only safe when it is coupled with keeping the faith that you are okay, and trusting yourself and life.

Give up hope of a better now.

If you are having an awful time, you may well feel it should have been different, and it should be different, and it is not okay, and it will never be okay, and you will never be okay. And yet you do need to say *Yes* to it anyway.

Saying *Yes* to life doesn't mean you are happy about it or see it in a positive light. It just means that you stop fighting the fact that it has happened or is happening, and acknowledge that you are not in charge here, and must surrender.

Again, I need to remind you to beware of that old 'control mind'. Surrender does not mean surrender to your belief about what this implies about you, your value or your future. The facts of what is happening – that your beloved has died, or that your marriage is over, or that you are unemployed – and your feelings of loss, fear, abandonment and anger are your reality right now.

So be it.

But your judgements and predictions about it – that you must have done something terribly wrong or that you will *never* be happy again or that someone must pay – are your control mind speaking. They are usually not only untrue, but they are also harmful to your wellbeing. Acknowledge these judgements and predictions, accept them and then let them go.

As you keep doing this, you will begin to realize that the events in your life have many possible meanings, and that by staying open, you will begin to discover some new ones that point out the way forward. This is what my neighbour Chris (see page 53) discovered and it catapulted her into her new life. So, of course, did Loraine, who decided to see the experience as her spiritual teacher.

I like to say to myself, 'There's nothing I need to be happy that I don't already have.' This never seems true at the time I believe I am missing the one thing I need for happiness, but it does always turn out to be true once I let go and turn to what is coming towards me rather than complain about what is not coming towards me.

What is coming towards *you* now that might bring you joy or nourishment or healing?

Give up hope of a better past.

Aba Gayle is an inspiring woman who works to help murderers on death row, including the man who murdered her daughter. She used to give out bumper stickers saying, *Forgiveness is Giving up all Hope of a Better Past.* This was what she herself had to do in order to forgive and move on from her despair, rage and bitterness about her daughter's murder and begin to live again.

Whom do you need to forgive? It may be yourself, or it may be another, and often it is life itself that you need to forgive. If only you, or someone else, or life itself, had been better, this would not have happened.

There are many reasons why you might not want to do so: You may blame yourself or feel someone else needs to learn a lesson, or feel that what happened is unfair, or be defending the rights of a loved one to have had better treatment.

Lucy, a member of one of my groups, told me she would never forgive her ex-husband because it would be wrong to forgive him what he did to her daughter, and he needed to be taught a lesson. As a result she, and probably her daughter, were stuck with him in their imagination, rather than being able to leave him behind and move on.

But forgiveness is not a one-step process; if we don't experience all the feelings first, including the anger, resentment and sadness, we cannot fully forgive.

Jane, another group member, talked to the group about how, at the age of 12, she found her mother's body just after her mother had shot herself. The scene is almost unimaginable. Yet Jane immediately forgave her mother, or so she told herself, and never felt any anger.

The only trouble was, Jane now had absolutely no memory of her childhood until that moment, and therefore no memory of her mother when she was alive. That is quite a punishment for the mother she 'forgave'.

I met a fascinating woman at a naturopathic clinic, where I was recovering from burnout, who gave me her formula for dealing with being hurt by others. She would say, 'F-you, and I put you in God's hands.' In other words: *Yes, I'm angry, but no, it is not my job to teach you a lesson.* It is a reminder that so often we refuse to forgive because we believe that the other person needs to learn that what they did is not okay.

I have passed this little mantra on to more people than I can remember and it usually brings a smile, and relief.

Often the place where our lack of forgiveness is held is in the feelings we have about life itself. It's a bit like that background feeling in a dream that can hang over you when you wake. You may forgive everyone in your life, and yet still feel angry or resentful or self-pitying in a vague background way that has to do with your feelings about life itself.

Of course, your earliest experiences of your family and your environment *were* life then, and it is only later that you separated out life itself from the particular people and situations in life. So at a primitive level, whatever happened early on may be hanging on in the form of your attitudes to life.

There is an exercise on forgiving life in the Spiritual Gym at the end of this chapter.

Give up hope of a better future

In the story about my father I told earlier (see page 71), my father, like Chris in the previous chapter, had not only to accept the present, but also to accept that he would never have the future he had hoped he would have. My father had hoped against hope that someday the people who had hurt him would say they were sorry and make amends. Chris had looked forward to a quiet retirement with her beloved husband. Death made this impossible for both of them in different ways.

Often the future we believed we would have is what we are really mourning. My client, Veronica, for example, was unable to let go of her mourning for her father, who she had in fact never got on with and had been angry at all her life.

Who was she mourning? She was mourning the father she never had, but had always hoped she would someday, when he would ask for forgiveness and treat her well.

My friend Julie, similarly, couldn't let go of mourning the break-up of her relationship with her girlfriend. What she was mourning was the 'happily ever after' she would never have.

At times when you need to make changes in your life, it becomes vital not to tie your happiness to a particular future.

Eventually, you will set an intention for what you want, and be willing to go for it wholeheartedly, not letting obstacles get in your way. But, even then, you need to let go of *having* to have it, and recognize that whatever happens, you are still okay. I call this double awareness 'intending and releasing' and we will look at it further when we get closer to new beginnings.

If you want a happy life, it just cannot depend on X and not Y happening, or you really are at the mercy of the forces of life and of your own limitations. You may *never* get whatever it is you thought was essential to your life or to your sense of self, and you will still be okay.

Keep the faith

This is where the *Keep the Faith* bit comes in. It refers to a kind of radical trust in yourself and in life, that you will still be there and basically okay no matter what. This is not a static state, but something about knowing that the sun will rise again and that there will be at least one more new beginning.

If you give up hope without knowing that you are still okay, still the same wonderful human being you always were, this is resignation, not acceptance.

Resignation is what happens when you give up hope, but your sense of who you are is still tied up with whatever it is you are giving up hope about. As a result, you feel you are losing part of yourself, becoming diminished, smaller.

Acceptance is what you do when you give up hope, but know that your true identity and value are still safe because they don't depend on whatever it is you are giving up hope about. Resignation will keep you stuck, while true acceptance will help you to move on.

Resignation is what happens if you fall on hard times, sell your expensive car and think that you have to accept that you are a failure. But if you fall on hard times and sell that same car, but discover a pride and joy about being able to live without your old status symbols, that is acceptance.

Miss Smilla, the main character in Peter Hoeg's novel *Miss Smilla's Feeling for Snow,* described how she kept the faith:

> *I'm not perfect. I think more highly of snow and ice than of love. It's easier for me to be interested in mathematics than to have affection for my fellow human beings. But I am anchored to something in life that is constant. You can call it a sense of orientation; you can call it woman's intuition; you can call it whatever you like. I'm standing on rock bottom and further than that I cannot fall.* [1]

Your Spiritual Gym
Exercise 4:
Forgiving Life

Materials: Imagework Diary and pen and paper.

1. Begin with a relaxation. Try any technique you like, such as the one in the *8 Tips to Harnessing your Imagination* on page 42, or try this shorter one: Close your eyes. Roll your eyes up to the ceiling. Forget your eyes. Notice any tension in your body. Say hello to it and smile. Forget your body. Imagine a big light above your head, larger than your shoulders, and pull it slowly through your body, imagining that everywhere it touches, it relaxes, softens, heals, brings peace and absorbs whatever doesn't benefit you. Finally, it sinks through your feet into the earth, depositing whatever it has absorbed to be transformed. Allow a lightness to come up from the ground through your whole body, and then out through the top of your head. Surrender. Let go and see what happens.

2. Take an empty chair and put it opposite you. Allow an image to emerge of Life and your relationship to it on the chair. How does Life look to you? How do you feel in its presence?

3. Tell Life all the things you feel, the good and the bad, including the rage and the fear and the abandonment or whatever comes up. Don't be reasonable. Just get into the worst of it and don't worry if you feel that

you are complaining. Complain to Life as bitterly as you can manage.

4. Switch seats, and become Life. Breathe into being Life. How does it feel to be Life? Look back at yourself, who I will now call Self. How does Self look to you? How do you feel in his or her presence? Did you hear what Self said? Now as Life say back to Self anything that comes to you.

5. Continue this conversation, both of you being brutally honest, until you really acknowledge to each other how the other feels. When you are ready, also say the things you appreciate and love about each other.

6. When you are ready, speaking as Self, forgive Life, and then switch roles and speaking as Life, forgive Self.

7. Let the love and appreciation flow between you.

8. Reflect on what has happened, and on what can now be different.

9. Write or draw or represent this experience in your Imagework Diary.

10. If you are still feeling a bit in a trance, count yourself up or have your buddy count you up: 'I'm going to count up from 1–5 and when I say 5 I'm going to open my eyes (you're going to open your eyes), relaxed and alert, bringing the peace and wisdom back with me (with you). 1–2-eyelids lightening, 3-4-coming to the surface,

5. Eyes open. I stamp my feet (stamp your feet) and come back to the room.' Three stamps.

Here's a conversation with Life that I myself had many years ago that I still remember because it really changed things for me. At a time when I was feeling disappointed about something that had happened – and I can't now even remember what it was – I imagined Life sitting opposite me and I started this conversation,

'Why is it that you give me everything but what I really want?'

Life responded by saying, 'Why is it that whatever I give you, you still complain?'

I had to laugh. Answering a question with a question is such a typical Jewish response.

We continued the conversation, and Life made clear to me that I took for granted everything that was going well in my life, and focused on the problems and lacks. In particular, I was taking for granted my wonderful relationship with my kids. I promised that I would do better.

That promise ushered in a beautiful phase of cherishing life with my kids, Ari and Chloe, who were then young teenagers. It is particularly wonderful to have done this, because though I somehow hadn't realized it, it wasn't long before they left home, and that phase was over forever. I was and am so very grateful for that special time we had together thanks to that conversation with Life.

CHAPTER 5

I'm Still There

Once you have been able to stop, give up hope and keep the faith, it is important to settle consciously into a new sense of who and what you are, a permanent experience of being you that you come back to even when everything else changes. This core sense of self, or central identity, must be resilient enough to go beyond all that you have lost or can lose.

My friend Tony Crisp is the person who taught me most about this. Tony and I were in the middle of writing a book together when he had a stroke that at first rendered him partially paralyzed and unable to speak at all. Tony was a writer, author of almost 20 books, including the bestselling *Dream Dictionary*,[1] as well as a yoga and bodywork teacher, so the speech and movement he had lost seemed absolutely central to who he was.

And yet, as Tony told me later when he had regained his speech, at that very moment when it seemed as if all was lost, he was trying desperately to communicate to us with his smile that he was okay because he was still there. His identity did not depend even on his brain.

Because he didn't have the language to tell us, and we didn't have the imagination to guess, we were all devastated. But he was okay and at peace.

Okay doesn't mean in full health; far from it. It simply meant that he hadn't lost himself, no matter what had happened to his brain. He was still there.

Interestingly enough, the spiritual teacher Ram Dass, called the book he completed after he had a major stroke *Still Here*[2].

Since then, Tony has mostly recovered, and is back to his computer, writing and helping people with their dreams. But he will never say that being healthy is a better state than lying in bed with a stroke. Nor is it worse. The important thing is that he is there.

In all my fears of the worst happening in my own life, I am reassured by Tony's experience of being hit by what seemed to all his friends to be the worst thing that could happen to him and staying so very peaceful. I have the inner knowledge that if I am still there, then on some level I will be okay, and somehow or other I will turn a corner to see a new and bigger vista.

And so will you.

WILL YOU RECOGNIZE YOURSELF ANYWHERE?

If you reflect upon it, I think you'll find that you already have an inner place you go to where you recognize yourself, where you know that 'This is me'. Indeed, you also know that there is something others recognize about you even when you think you have changed.

I remember coming back from a year as a student in Israel and appearing at my university feeling I had become a new and different person, only to be greeted by my quirky English Literature professor announcing in his sonorous tones, 'Dina Glouberman, you haven't changed a bit. That means to say: I would recognize you *anywhere*.'

What a disappointment it was… and yet, how reassured I also felt.

WHAT KIND OF STABILITY ARE WE TALKING ABOUT?

It is not enough simply to have a place inside where you recognize yourself. It is important to go further, to find or create or imagine an inner space that has the qualities you need as you step out of difficult times towards new beginnings – the qualities that offer you the possibility of a true turning point.

Which qualities must this sense of yourself have? It must be so *stable* that you are safe no matter what you may lose, so *creative* that you know that you can meet change with your own adaptability and your powerful imagination, and so *connected* that you know that you are not alone, and that you are part of something larger than yourself. It must also have the ring of *love, meaning* and *truth* about it for you to trust that you are being guided towards your highest and your best. And it must include the awareness that you always have a *choice* about how to respond to life, no matter what life has thrown at you.

Victor Frankl, who wrote about what he learned through his experience of being in a concentration camp in his wonderful book *Man's Search for Meaning*, said this: 'Everything can be taken from a man but one thing: The last of human freedoms – to choose one's attitude in any given set of circumstances, to choose one's own way.'[3]

When you find or create or imagine this self, learn to access it at will, and begin to identify with it as you, then losses will not mean you have lost yourself, changes will not mean that you may be left stranded and unable to cope, and choices will not be made only for yourself but also for others.

Why do I say, 'find or create or imagine'? This is because I don't want you to get sidetracked into thinking that if you don't believe in an essential self, or a stable self, or a soul, or anything else, this is not going to work for you.

If you do believe in something like this, as I do in fact, then this work will help you to access and utilize it. But if you don't, you can still create or imagine an inner space that can work for you, and that can even eventually become a recognizable part of yourself. In the meantime, you can 'act as if' this is you, an approach that will help you to leap forward immeasurably without being untrue to your core beliefs.

Does stability mean that you can get stuck in bad situations? Paradoxically, the ability to remain the same is what makes it safe enough to risk change. And change we must, because it is in our nature to adapt and change and to shape change around us.

One of my group members in Skyros talked about her fear of gaining roots because then she would be well and truly stuck in a situation she wasn't happy about. We were working with an image of her being a plant and suddenly she felt those roots. Against all rhyme and reason, but with great jubilation, she cried out, 'I've got roots. Now I can move!'

LET'S CALL IT THE SOUL
When I work with people to help them find, create or

imagine a core sense of self that will protect and guide them, I give them an image of a large light behind them, larger than life itself, and I say, 'Let's call it the soul.' Because everyone knows what light is, and many have a sense of what a soul might be, this seems to work very well even for people who have no spiritual beliefs.

Most people that I have interviewed do have a felt sense of something that goes beyond everyday life, or a concept of the soul. They use words like: *My true self, my values, the eternal part of me, my highest and best purpose, my creative spark, my love, my human spirit, the part of me that knows, my essence, my being.*

Do any of these have significance for you, even if you wouldn't personally think of it as the soul? If not, perhaps you could just think of the soul as your wisdom self, that part of you that you rely on when you need inner guidance and direction. Or perhaps your integrity, that bit of you that you believe you should stand by when all else fails, or your ability to love, or your will. Or your highest or deepest or biggest consciousness. Or find some other meaning that works for you.

The important thing is that it must be an aspect of you that doesn't depend on your present circumstances, achievements or possessions, but is rather a more stable sense of who you are that protects and guides you in life.

Whatever you believe in, I hope you won't mind if I refer to this element as the soul. The soul, as it is generally understood, operates according to a different set of meanings than your everyday personality. The soul's meanings are more to do with being and loving and wisdom and contribution to others and what life is all about, while the everyday personality is more concerned with control, success, approval, managing the status quo, meeting emotional needs and achieving personal goals.

We need both, of course. Our everyday personality is what enables us to live in this world effectively, but if we accept the guidance of the soul's love and wisdom in doing so we have an inner compass and a sense of home that guides us towards our highest and our best.

Try this: *Imagine a big light behind you right now, larger than life itself. Lean back or step back into the light, and imagine that you become that light. Breathe into being that light. What does it feel like, what are your qualities, and what are you able to do? Light has many aspects – energy, lightness, strength, truth, love, presence and so on. Find out what it feels like for you. Is this feeling familiar in any way? Still being the light, look back at your normal self and your life. How do you look? What can you see that your normal self doesn't know?*

Once you have a sense of how to become this big light, it becomes a vantage point from which you can look at yourself and your life with more objectivity and wisdom than you normally have when caught up in everyday life. When in trouble, you just learn to step back into the light and find peace. You can then use this light every day to make your life and your work easier, and to let go slowly but surely of those attitudes that no longer honour you or life.

The power of soul esteem

As you develop a sense of something that goes beyond the everyday personality, you may find that concepts like self esteem become less relevant. This is because self esteem is usually based on feeling good about your everyday personality. I like to talk of soul esteem, which is another thing entirely.

The concept of soul esteem emerged for me when I was giving a talk to participants and staff about the history of setting up Skyros holidays. I had decided that this time instead of writing a short talk, I would just open up and be fully present and see what came up.

I found myself telling them that when we started Skyros, I had no self esteem at all. I was a mixed-up young woman, who had taken on more than she thought she could manage. I always imagined that people came to Skyros because of all the famous people we invited, and I was the janitor or caretaker that held it all together. I still remember when Stewart, one of the teaching staff, said to me, 'We come because we love you.' I practically looked around to see whom he was talking to! It took years for me to understand that other people valued me and took me seriously when I didn't.

But what I had was soul esteem. And soul esteem was the knowledge that if my soul was whispering for me to do something I would do it, and I wouldn't wonder if I was worthy, and I wouldn't count the cost.

As soon as I really saw and took on the vision of Skyros, and knew this was the right thing to do at this moment in our lives, nothing could stop me.

This was not because I was so confident.

Confidence didn't come into it.

And it was not because it went so smoothly that it must be 'meant to be'. In fact, at certain points it seemed as if everything was going wrong. I used to comfort myself with the idea in the *I Ching,* the Chinese book of wisdom, 'Difficulty at the beginning works supreme success.'[4]

No, it was because if it was on my plate to do, I would do it if it was in my power to do so, and that was that. From what I have seen and understood of creative people, this approach is very common. Many creative people have no self esteem, may even fall apart when they are not creating, but when it becomes clear to them that there is something they must do, nothing will stop them. This is soul esteem.

COMPASSION FOR YOUR LIMITATIONS AND RESPECT FOR YOUR MAGNIFICENCE

So the trick at this turning point moment is not to try too hard to gain the confidence you've never had, but to choose radical trust rather than mistrust. Know that your soul or your essential self will guide you even when personally you may feel lost, and then wait for a vision or an understanding or a feeling that shows you which way to go, one which you cannot say no to. Then, success or failure are just information that tells you how to proceed.

When you are struggling and feeling bad about yourself and life, you may find it difficult to believe that you can trust yourself to be guided to your highest and your best. It is characteristic of the thinking in our culture that you must be either strong or weak, either wonderful or awful, either confident or terrified. We forget that there is more to us than this, and that we can be both at the same time.

This is the nature of being human.

We need to discover the magical power of a truly respectful and loving way to look at ourselves and others. We must see us all with compassion for our pain or limitations, and, at one and the same time, respect for our magnificence. Only then can we fully honour our humanity.

Try this: *Think of someone you really care about and value who may be going through difficult times. Picture that person, see the look on their face, and look at them consciously with love and compassion for their pain and limitations, and also respect for their magnificence. Does their expression change? And is it clear to you at this moment that at one and the same moment he or she may feel lost, rudderless and in pain, and yet on another level be a wonderful being with unlimited potential? Now try looking at yourself in the same way!*

The combination of compassion and respect, the ability to do both of these at the same time, is the secret to remembering who you really are even when the going gets tough.

***Try this:** Think of a time when you have felt really bad about yourself, and really closed down. Perhaps it is right this minute! If not, remember it vividly. Or even think of a fear of the future you have that makes you tense up and contract. When you have felt this fully, imagine there is a light opposite you, which we will call the soul. Now switch into being that light, looking back at Self, and sending Self your love, including compassion for his or her pain and limitation and respect for his or her magnificence. You might also say something like, 'I am sorry you are suffering, and I also see what an amazing being you are, and I love you.' Keep doing this until Self really gets it and perks up or expands or smiles. Now switch back and be Self and see how you feel.*

Our wisdom self is not difficult to access but unless we practise staying in contact with it, our awareness will be like a flabby muscle that doesn't work for us.

By practising regularly seeing life from the point of view of the big light, which I am calling the soul, you will find that you have a wonderful resource no matter what you believe in.

There is an old saying that 'the soul makes everything new'. What could be more perfect when you are moving through your turning point towards new beginnings?

Your Spiritual Gym

Exercise 5:

Biography of Self and Soul

Materials needed: Your Imagework Diary, a pen, and oil pastels or crayons. For the written part of this exercise, you may find it easier to work at your computer.

1. Write at the top of the page: **(Your name's) Brief Autobiography** (e.g. John's Brief Autobiography). Then start to write in a stream of consciousness the story of your life to the present day. It doesn't have to be representative. Just see what comes up. It can be as short or as long as you like, but try to keep it to 5 or 10 minutes.

2. Write at the top of the next page: **The Soul's Brief Biography of (your name).** Now imagine there is a big light behind you, larger than life itself, which we will call the soul, and step back into it and become the light. Now start to write the story of your life from the point of view of the soul, again probably for not much more than 5 or 10 minutes and without planning.

3. How are these stories different? Are they both true? Which story is a more helpful and kind way of seeing your life?

4. If you believed the soul's version, what would be different?

5. You might also do a picture of the two different views of self. I recommend doing them on separate pages, and then holding them up to the light to see how they fit together.

CHAPTER 6
Expand Don't Contract

When I interviewed the late Gabrielle Roth, founder of the worldwide Five Rhythms dance movement, about her turning points in life, she told me this story about how she came to a new and expanded sense of herself at a painful moment.

Little Miss Goody Two Shoes saved herself for the 'big prince'. The first time I made love, I got pregnant. I was 18. But the prince rode off on his horse in the opposite direction. I cried, and fell apart, was in despair.

Then I woke up and was myself. I realized that the fairy tale was over and I was free. This guy was a scared young man, totally freaked out. His freak-out catalyzed my transformation… and I rode off into the night by myself. I took charge of my own sexual existence.[1]

For Gabrielle, being in charge of her own sexuality meant she knew who she was, and she didn't have to fall apart every time a man disappointed or abandoned her. She expanded into a real freedom. Her sexual transformation also became the basis of everything that she gave to people all around the world.

British actor Michael York had a very different kind of expansion – an opening up to alternative therapies and to his spirituality. He told me this story when I asked him about his turning point in life:

A turning point in my life came in India. I was there with Pat. Both of us had always taken life for granted. But suddenly she became very, very ill and was given a 5 per cent chance of survival. I had just proposed to her – and three days later she was dying. I found myself signing papers that meant I was taking responsibility for her life.

She survived, and we got married two days after we came back from India. I think I saw how fragile human existence is; one minute you are planning the future very happily and in love, and the next moment the future has a big question mark or maybe there is no future.

It had a profound effect on me; it heightened my sensibilities enormously. I got interested in various alternative therapies and started tapping into a spiritual side, which I found coming more and more to the fore. It's been an ongoing thing, like peeling layers of an onion, and the more you peel the more there is left. And I'm still searching, keeping all doors open.[2]

If the first step out of difficult times is to stop and accept the reality of how it is, how it has been, and how it may be in future, and the second step is to find that in you that is stable, creative and connected no matter what happens, the third step is to use that security to expand and refocus, to find out what your soul is whispering, and be willing to trust it. In a sense, it is all about saying *Yes*, not just to your present reality, but to life itself, to your deepest self, and to what may be.

CONTRACTING

There is a natural and useful reaction of contraction in a crisis that means that you are equipped to fight, flee or freeze. Your energy is focused, hopefully you are also open to receiving energy and appropriate help from the world around you, and you go for it. When you have achieved your goal or have come to resolution, you can expand again into relaxation and joy.

But contraction doesn't always work that way. This is particularly so if you need a turning point, i.e. you don't actually know what to do for the best, and need to open up to a new understanding rather than close down prematurely.

If you aren't dealing with an immediate physical emergency, and the fight/flight/freeze response is not appropriate, you may find yourself contracting in a different and more emotional way, feeling tense, frightened, overwhelmed, depressed, hopeless or helpless. This kind of contraction is a kind of collapsing in on yourself, and can hang around in your system and cause trouble. It is particularly counter to everything you need to have a turning point.

I remember how when I was 27, I thought I was really old and past it and I was just never going to achieve what I had hoped. I started to hunch my shoulders as if I were old, wrote letters headed by a date in the past, and even found myself mistakenly giving as my telephone number the one I had had years before. I then proceeded to get very depressed.

I was well and truly stuck, contracted and moving backwards.

Luckily, this phase came to an end before too long and I felt young again. Since then, I have noticed that throughout life, I keep getting old and then young again, and it has little to do with which decade I am in. It is all about the cycle of contraction and expansion.

Think for a moment of how you feel in your body when you are frightened, stressed or overwhelmed. Notice how tension builds up. This is literally a contraction of certain muscles. Similarly on an emotional level, you may feel anxious and/or depressed, and you might close down, curl up in a ball, retreat, perhaps feeling very young and helpless. Mentally, you might be having repetitive thought loops that go round and round without really getting anywhere.

If you imagined an energy field around you, it would be small and collapsed and closed to outside influences. You are neither flowing in nor out towards others or towards the world; you are neither sending nor receiving love or positive energy. Nothing is too small for you to fail at it.

Not only that, but it will be obvious to others by the way you stand and move and hold your body that all is not well. I remember walking into a room to meet my friend Raj, and before I opened my mouth, he said, 'You look defeated.'

When you are contracted, you aren't able to operate in a free and creative way, or to be in touch with the kind of resources you need for larger life decisions. Moreover, on a physical level, because contraction has a big impact on how you stand and move, certain body patterns will begin to fix themselves and become rock solid, bringing with them tension, pain or illness.

Of course, it is often the times that you most need your

resources that you have a contraction response. Think of the times you feel it is absolutely urgent to do or decide something and yet are feeling unable to do or decide anything creatively and effectively.

WHEN DO YOU CONTRACT?

The challenges that fell you are usually those that hit a vulnerable part of you, an Achilles heel. It may be to do with your self esteem, your emotional investments, your pride, your identity or your perfectionism. Whatever it is, what happens when you collapse, or move backward, or get tense or depressed, is that you lose all contact with who you really are, and what is really possible.

My friend Joan always feels hopeless around money. She's never had much money, never felt she was any good at making, keeping or managing it, and has a deep sense of failure in this area. So if she has financial difficulties, all these feelings come up and she immediately gets in a panic, hides her head in an ostrich-like fashion and feels totally helpless. When she has problems with men, on the other hand, she is confident, and knows she can sort it out, and if this man doesn't work out, another will come along. Needless to say her problems with money don't get sorted, but those with men do.

Another friend, Alison, is exactly the opposite; money issues don't faze her because she knows she is confident and good at dealing with them, but man problems knock her sideways because all her feelings of failure come up, and she collapses in a heap pretty quickly, and deals with things really badly.

Get to know yourself: What kind of challenge do you meet with all your colours flying, and before which do you falter and give up hope? And which type is going on right now if this is a difficult time for you?

And if this is one of those Achilles heel ones, how can you step forth into a positive future when you feel that you will never manage it, you're not good at it, nobody would ever believe you and you don't believe yourself? You've shot yourself in the foot before you even started.

EXPANDING

The trick at these moments is to recognize that you *are* collapsed, and find a way through to an expanded self. If you look back at Gabrielle Roth's story at the beginning of this chapter, you will see her moving through her collapse to an expanded sense, as she 'rides off into the night'.

Think now for a moment of how you feel in your body when you are confidently moving forward, doing something you love and that you know you are good at. Your muscles relax, your emotions, and indeed your whole energy field, are open and flowing. Your mind is creative, ideas come easily, decisions can be made freely from your strengths and not your weaknesses, and you can send and receive love. You sense that this wonderful energy is flowing through you, rather than having to feel that you are a wonderful special one.

In this state of mind, also, it is possible to move to another level of yourself, to take your next step in understanding and in action. Nothing is too big to undertake if the time is right and the project is appropriate. You have expanded.

CHANGING GEAR

When you realize that you are contracted, for whatever reason, this is not a time to rush out and do something fast; the most urgent thing is to keep breathing and come back to your normal expanded self. Once you have come back to yourself, you will be able to do what you have to do or decide what you have to decide so much more effectively.

Think of it as if someone has stuck a spear in you; no matter how hurt and angry you feel it is best, if at all possible, not to rush out to battle with the spear in you, but to retreat, take out the spear, heal as much as possible, and then go back out to fight with strength and presence of mind.

Picture yourself in a situation which hits your Achilles heel, or perhaps you are in one right now. Do you feel big or small? Grown up, very old or very young? Chances are you are feeling small, young or very old, helpless, at the mercy of whatever it is that is coming at you. You are contracted.

What would it take for you to switch gears from contracted to even a tiny bit expanded?

There are many ways to do this, from physical changes to insight to imagination. You may have your own favourite activity or meditation or breathing techniques or inspiring music or friend to talk to that works for you. Or here are some quickish ones that work for me. Try them out first when you are feeling okay and see which seems to be most effective.

Nothing works all the time, so it's good to have a few strings in your bow. Sometimes a combination of two or three is magic.

◆

Try these:
Just say to yourself: '*Expand, don't contract!*'
Now look at yourself in your mind's eye – or, even better, look at yourself in a mirror – with that look we spoke of in the last chapter that includes compassion for your limitations and respect for your magnificence. And imagine giving yourself a big hug and saying, 'You're great, and I love you.'

Stepping back: *Imagine there is a large light behind you, larger than life itself. Step back into the light, even imagine being the light. Stay in the light, or be the light, for as long as you can while you walk, talk and carry out your daily activities.*

An energy approach: *Imagine that you have a bubble all around you that is your energy field. You can picture it as a bubble of light. Now open it up at the top, and ask for and imagine a power shower of light flowing down through you, washing you with light and pushing down the heavy energy, i.e. all that is in the way of your wellbeing, into the earth to be transformed. Now ask for and imagine some nourishing light coming up from the earth, flooding you with good energy. Release the light through that opening at the top of your energy bubble. See this as a flow-through down and up, where you wash yourself with light, empty out the heavy energy and get nourished by the light energy. (This is an adaptation of a technique of the Inca people.)*

Breathe: *Breathe three times slowly in and out from the abdomen and imagine sending energy down to your feet. Now imagine expanding into a bigger picture of yourself.*

A physical activity: *Stamp your feet, go for a walk, or run, or dance or bicycle. It is always useful to extend or expand yourself physically, and to ground yourself in this way very literally through your connection with the ground.*

An emotional approach: *Take care of the child in you, and then contact the strength and resourcefulness of the adult. Here's one way: Get an image of a child, your own inner child, see how old he or she is, and notice how he or she is feeling. Now say to the child, 'This is hard, and it's going to be okay, and I love you and I think you're amazing.' And then ask yourself, 'And as an adult, what do I need to do?'*

A cognitive insight approach: *Accept the fact that you have collapsed and question why. Is it based on some false belief? Uncover the false belief about yourself or about life that has just been shattered, and ask yourself about your real truth.*

Here's an example of this from a recent experience of mine. There was a moment a couple of years ago when I realized that everything I had attempted for the last six months had gone nowhere. I felt low, discouraged, contracted.

Talking to my friend Silke about it, I found myself saying, 'Everything I've tried has failed. Maybe that was my success.' As soon as I said it, I realized that this was true. I'd been barking up the wrong tree, pushing for results that weren't right for me, then feeling like a failure, instead of patiently waiting for what was really coming towards me. This was my turning point. I stopped, let go of my plans, stopped feeling like a failure and, before long, something new showed up in my life that did work out for me.

Transferring skills: *Picture yourself in a situation where you are or have been expanded and confident. Step into the picture and breathe into being that person. Then turn to look at your present self and find out how to deal with your situation from this perspective. Remember: You are what you imagine.*

Heart and soul esteem: *If you are contracted because of low self-confidence, you need to find what your heart and soul are whispering, and simply follow it, without asking yourself if you are good enough. This is heart and soul esteem.*
Go into your heart and ask what your heart is saying. Are you willing to listen? Step into that light of the soul we worked with in the last chapter and look at the situation and find a new way forward.

Expand your energy field: *See yourself in your*

imagination with a small ball of light around you, like a tiny energy field made of light. How big is it right now? Now imagine the light ball is as big as the room, then as your city, then as your country. Breathe deeply and stay present. Has something changed?

You and the Solar System: *Vividly imagine the whole solar system and its vastness in whatever way feels real and true to you. Now, become aware of yourself, and your consciousness, as a tiny part of that solar system. (When I did this exercise, I expected to feel small, but instead I felt expanded, as if my consciousness was the same size as the universe. Find out how it works for you.)*

The good old-fashioned way: *Talk to friends. Tell them the truth about what happened and about your feelings. Ask for their perspective. Let yourself remember that no matter what happened, in the eyes of your friends you are still okay, loveable and as amazing as ever.*

CAN YOU BE TOO EXPANDED?

To complicate matters, it can easily happen that you go to the other extreme and become too expanded. At the opposite end of contraction is over-expansion. You can be so expanded, you practically step off the ground. This is why they call this 'being high'. Some of us don't need drugs to get high!

At these moments you experience yourself as bigger than life, inexhaustible, invincible. There is nothing you cannot do, no barrier you cannot overcome. Your creativity is flowing, but rather than seeing it as a gift that flows through you, you see yourself as the ultimate creative one, the rescuer, the knight in shining armour, the superhero. You may feel that you are the only one, the special one, that one who is chosen to do this or that. Have you ever felt like this?

It's always amazing how, in response to your state of mind, your history rewrites itself, and so does your imagined future. When you are contracted and low, not only are you helpless now, but all you can remember are the times in your life when you have felt like that, and all you can predict is that you will feel like that forever. But when you are invincible, your life is a series of victories over adversity, and in future you will become even more powerful and unstoppable.

In this state of over-expansion, even though your creativity and energy seem to be flowing, your judgement can be poor, your view of yourself and others may be distorted, you can deplete your energy quickly, and you may find it too easy to step forward in a foolhardy way, even into danger.

I was definitely prone to switching between these opposites until I understood what was happening. I remember times when I got so high, I practically believed I could heal the sick and raise the dead. Then, of course, when I found that I was limited, made mistakes, couldn't perform miracles, the bubble would burst and I would get depressed. If I was not extraordinary, I was nothing.

At their best, my highs were full of wonderful insights, great spiritual experiences, wondrous understandings about myself and others. But my lows lasted so much longer, and were so very tough.

THE GOLDEN PATH BETWEEN THE OPPOSITES

Slowly I began to understand that neither highs nor lows brought me comfort or lasting truth, and that if I could keep to the middle path, I could stand in my power, authority and wisdom. Moreover, I could do it solidly, patiently, persistently and with joy. This is being centred.

You may not be fully aware that neither pole is good, because invincible feels so much better than being helpless and hopeless. But, in fact, neither extreme is a solid grounded position. Both are illusions. It turns out that it is the level road down the middle that gets you where you are going a lot faster and with fewer mishaps.

Being high and invincible actually doesn't feel good to me anymore, and I always try to get back to centre as soon as I can.

In my experience, both of these poles are tied up with an unrealistically high expectation of yourself, coupled with the secret belief that you are unworthy. In fact, being a superhero is your minimum proof that you are okay! When things go really well, it feels both thrilling and unbelievable. You have achieved what on one level you believed was impossible. You deal with this by getting high, hoping against hope this is proof that you really are okay after all, indeed that all will be well forever, and you are uniquely amazing and protected.

It is as if you have filled yourself like a balloon, tied the end so the good feelings don't escape and, as a result, are flying high.

Then if things go badly, or just not as fantastically as you expected, hope fails, the balloon is pricked and falls to the ground. Suddenly, you are nothing and no one.

In the high there is life and no death, and in the low there is death and no life.

What you are unable to do in this scenario is to simply keep breathing in and out, whether you are succeeding or failing, knowing that you are okay no matter what.

If these are not your opposites, there may well be other opposites. For example, my client Kathy was dealing with the death of her mother as well as with her own terminal illness. She veered between closing down completely so as to feel nothing, or being so overwhelmed by all her feelings that she became anxious and unable to cope. Neither position supported her and those around her to find her truth and her real options.

In my research with people who burned out, this veering between the two opposites is often a 'normal' part of everyday life. The highs feel great and give the adrenaline you need to accomplish great things well beyond normal limits, but when you crash and burn, you have nothing to sustain you. You are exhausted and often feel empty.

In the terms of the old fairy tale about the goose that lay the golden eggs, when you are high, you value yourself for the golden eggs you produce, and when you are low, you are nothing but a rather pathetic sad goose.

Highly creative people – who are often prone to burnout – frequently do this veering between the two extremes, where they either feel helpless, hopeless and small, or else feel invincible, invulnerable and able to overcome anything. I have noticed that many of my most successful and go-getting clients have this dynamic.

But when they are really at their best, they are doing neither. They are simply walking their walk and talking their talk with confidence and creativity. They are centred, walking the path between the opposites.

What is centre? It is a natural expanded and yet grounded place where you can act from your strengths and support yourself in your limitations, where your judgement is good and your vision is inspired. Unlike during your highs and lows, you can just keep breathing in and out whatever happens. You have come back to yourself.

I myself can sometimes feel this palpably, as if my sense of self is just flowing back into me. It always feels wonderful.

The first step towards getting centred is to be aware that this *is* a fluctuation between opposites, that you've been on both sides, and that you need to get to centre. Just this awareness can dislodge you from the certainty that what you are feeling is so real it cannot be questioned or doubted.

Next you need to consciously get yourself back to centre. Try saying *So be it* and then bringing yourself back to centre. But do also make use of the beautiful exercise in this chapter's Spiritual Gym called *The Golden Path Between the Opposites*. I find this one works every time for me and for my clients and students.

You are part of something

If you are not to get over-expanded, it does help to

remember that whatever it is you are doing is part of a larger picture.

Yes, you are hopefully choosing to do something you love doing, and to get the rewards that come with it. Yes, what you have chosen to do may well be contributing enormously to the world. On another level, however, you are playing your part, but you are not the whole show.

It is a rule of thumb that if you are seeing yourself as single-handedly saving the world, or even your world, you are probably caught in illusion and are at one pole or another. Illusions can become dangerous whether you succeed and over-expand, becoming a bit messianic, or you fail and contract, becoming hopeless and depressed.

It is not a time for Superman or Superwoman. You are a member of a team, even if you don't know all the members.

In my work on burnout, I have found that this understanding can mean the difference between burning out and burning on. Superman is bound to fail someday, whereas someone who is a team member can just learn a new role if the old one doesn't work.

What is the larger picture? In an immediate way it might be the family or group you are part of. Or it might be the people all over the world who are working towards positive goals. And on another level, we are part of the interconnected web that includes all of humanity, the planet and all its inhabitants.

Our largest truth always includes a connection to that which goes beyond our personal selves. I love the words of Rabbi Hillel, *If I am not for myself, who will be for me? And when I am only for myself what am I? And if not now, when?*

SOMETIMES YOU NEED A LITTLE HELP

Where possible, I work with my own process through imagery, and encourage others to do the same. My inspiration to create Imagework was my desire to be a teacher rather than a therapist, teaching people how to be their own therapists and healers, and I learned about this by doing it myself.

But that said, I often find I need other people's perspectives, and the skills that others have gained in their own art, which I may simply not have. So if you're sensing that you just can't find your way to expansion by yourself, please don't hesitate to find someone you trust, personally or professionally, and get help.

Here's a time when I was in pain, but didn't know why, and got the help I needed. It was all about contraction:

When my friend John was dying, I managed to be with him during his last days, and just after, though I was not present at the moment of death. It was terribly painful but it also felt like a privilege to go through this with him.

Soon after, I started having a painful neck, to the extent that I couldn't turn my head around. I visited two very good osteopaths who reassured me that this was normal 'wear and tear' due to age, and I could ameliorate it with exercise but I was more or less stuck with it.

I just didn't believe them. Why now?

Then I went to see my cranial osteopath, Gez Lamb, who has known me for over 20 years. Cranial osteopaths work with a more subtle level of the body and mind. I told him what the osteopaths had said and he looked at me and smiled, 'I've never known you to have anything that was purely physical.'

He found my heart was contracted, literally physically, and did one of his clicking manoeuvres to open the heart. As he left the room to let it settle, I could sense John's presence in my heart area. I realized I had unconsciously closed my heart around my sense of John's presence so as not to lose him, and that this contraction had changed my posture enough to lead to this pain in my neck.

So I whispered to John that I was willing now to let go, I wished him well, and asked him to fly away freely. That sense I had of John's presence around my heart dissolved.

Over the next few weeks, the 'wear and tear' pain disappeared, and has never returned.

Your Spiritual Gym
Exercise 6:
The Golden Path Between the Opposites

Materials needed: Your Imagework Diary or paper you can draw on, crayons and oil pastels. You will need three pieces of paper, or three pages in your diary.

1. Do a quick relaxation. For example: Breathe three times slowly and think of something that makes you feel peaceful and expanded. Now breathe three times slowly and imagine sending energy down to your feet. Now give yourself a moment to settle into a bigger sense of yourself.

2. Think of two opposite states of mind you veer between, perhaps being amazing and invincible vs. feeling like nothing, or being perfectly good vs. being perfectly bad, or being completely shut down vs. being completely overwhelmed by your feelings, or having run your life perfectly vs. having made one mistake after another. Where are you with this right now? Or start with how you feel and think at your worst, and then think of the opposite extreme; notice that you might find it easier to think of your worst self-accusations than to admit to your secret super-positive beliefs. Another way to figure this out is to think about something you feel bad about right now, and consider the underlying extreme beliefs. For example, if right now you feel you are an awful and selfish friend, do you perhaps tend

to think that if you are not perfectly good you must be perfectly selfish? Even if you really can't think of any opposites, move on to the next step and ask the image to help you.

3. Imagine that in the room there are two mountains, and between them is a golden path. See or sense where they are in the room. Name the mountains, or if you haven't figured out what your opposites are, ask each mountain what it is and see what comes up.

4. Go to one of the mountains, and walk around it in circles, or go in circles up the mountain, whichever feels more comfortable. Talk to yourself, if possible out loud, and just say all the things you think when you are in that state of mind. It's like having a dramatic monologue. For example, you might be berating yourself for being so stupid and useless and making so many mistakes, even telling yourself just to give up.

5. Now go to the other mountain, and do the same. Notice what comes up on this mountain. For example, you might be saying to yourself that you are absolutely great, probably better than anyone around you, and it is your job to save the world.

6. Now take the path in the middle, which is a golden path. You walk very slowly on this path between the mountains, doing a walking meditation, which means breathing out with your first step, and breathing in with your second step. And as you walk slowly, focusing on

your breathing, let yourself become aware of what it is like to be on this path and how the world looks. You may discover that on this path, just breathing, just being, just living, just loving is enough. If you find that you are quite wobbly, this is probably a sign that this middle path is very unfamiliar. If you feel as if you are walking a tightrope, imagine that the golden path is a wide avenue. Tell yourself, 'The path is wide.'

7. Take three pieces of paper or use three pages in your Imagework Diary. On the first page, think of the first mountain and express it in colour, finishing by writing a few words. Do the same for the second mountain and for the golden path. You might also want to write the story of the two mountains and the golden path between in your Imagework Diary.

8. Appreciate yourself for taking this journey and reflect on what it means, and how you can make use of your experience to stay more centred in future. How would your life be different if you were walking the golden path? You might say to yourself, 'If I walked the golden path, I would…'

9. Since it's probably impossible for most of us to stay on the golden path all the time, how do you remind yourself to get back on track as soon as you realize you have veered off? I find I can sometimes just picture the two mountains and then imagine walking the golden path, and get a sense of what that means, without actually physically going through the whole exercise. This helps if I am in a public place!

CHAPTER 7

Visioning for Dummies

The story so far: Difficult times come in all shapes and sizes, and they do come to an end if you trust yourself and life, honour your feelings, find that part of you that is still there whatever happens, and remember to expand, instead of just contracting and digging a deep hole and staying there.

Now you are hopefully ready to look around the corner, and see what you can see. It is time to get a sense of what your way forward can be, and to make some choices. Soon you will even get as far as turning the corner!

FASTEN YOUR SEAT BELT

Before you start doing any visioning of the future, it may help to do a bit of a checklist of where you have got to so far:

- Have you acknowledged that these have been difficult times, if they have been, but that the difficult feelings won't go on forever?
- Have you accepted that you can't change the past, you can't control the present, and that you may *never* have the thing you believe your happiness depends on?
- Do you get that you can still be okay?
- Have you seen that every time you let go of being contracted or over-expanded, there is a golden path that is safe for you to take?

♦ Have you sensed that beyond your self esteem, whether it is high or low, there is soul esteem, a knowledge that once you listen deeply to that part of you that is wisest, and see your next step, you will take it?

♦ Have you seen that you don't have to be Superman or Superwoman, perfect or extraordinary, in order to take this step?

♦ Have you been able to see yourself with real love, which includes compassion for your limitations and respect for your magnificence at one and the same time?

♦ Have you also got it that your happiness does not depend on your succeeding at anything at all, but just on remembering who you are and showing willing?

♦ Have you recognized, even vaguely, that at this very moment there are people all over the world having difficult times, aspiring to dreams, risking, succeeding and failing, and that you are all part of something larger than yourselves?

All of this is to say: Have you fastened your seat belt? Are you up for an adventure? Can you take a risk, go to a new destination, and deal with it if you get lost or fail? If so, you are safe. It is time to move into envisioning the future that is most in line with the whisperings of your wisdom mind, heart and soul, and find out how to get there.

Suzy's story

Mark's story of visioning (see page 35) was a good example of the power of inviting images of the future. You might want to go back to have a look. Here's another quite different one: My daughter-in-law Suzy's story…

Two years ago, my son and his family moved to Switzerland. As they planned the move, I was talking to Suzy about how her life was about to change dramatically, and what hopes and fears this change held for her. I suggested we could do a visioning to help her make the most of her new life. This would be a very new experience for her, but she was willing to go for it.

I recently asked her to write to me and tell me how it had worked out. This was her account:

Dina helped me envision my new life, and to focus on two alternative realities: One where I felt fulfilled and happy, and one where I was unhappy, lost and lonely. By doing this we identified how I may end up at both these alternative realities, and therefore how best to steer clear of one while heading positively and actively in the direction of the other.

I mainly feared not making connections, not finding time for myself in the myriad tasks of setting up my new life and home with two children and without much knowledge of the local language, and also feeling personally unfulfilled due to a lack of any creative outlet.

I saw I needed to actively prioritize reaching my positive reality – to step out of my comfort zone and seek people out rather than wait for someone to knock on my door, to focus on getting some help with the children so that I could free up a bit of time for myself, and to explore a creative outlet I had let fall by the wayside, my enjoyment of singing.

Two years on I sit and write this, and with good fortune and having been open to new experiences I can confidently say that I avoided my negative alternative reality and am up to now very much rooted in my positive one.

I have been very lucky to meet good and warm-hearted people, but I definitely feel that by having my personal goals orientated from the outset, I have avoided following paths that would have led me to dead ends. I have thrown myself into areas that have created opportunities and lasting friendships and that also enabled me to create my own reality.

With a good friend, I have set up a ladies group where we meet, chat and drink a glass of something while singing together. I never imagined I would have done that two years ago.

I have lost count of the number of people that have said, 'You seem to have settled in so quickly' or 'It feels like you've been here much longer' or 'It took me a good year before I felt like I had anyone to really talk to.' This last statement has simply not been the case for me. I am content in my life and through knowing what I needed to achieve in order to feel this way, at this moment in time I feel fulfilled.

What has had a lasting impact on me is the idea of seeing a turning point coming towards you and anticipating the fall-out before it happens. I always associated the need for guidance and help with such life changes to be in the aftermath of an untoward event or trauma, or because I was unable to cope with whatever new circumstances were thrown in my path. What Dina's work showed me was that the opposite was also true. Prepare yourself and allow yourself to be in control of the ride you see before you, even if you're not quite sure where it's headed.

This is a great description from someone who was completely new to visioning, and indeed to Imagework, of what visioning is all about and how it can make a real difference.

VISIONING IS NOT GOAL-SETTING

There is a big difference between setting a goal and sensing a vision. It has to do with which part of you is showing the way forward.

Goal-setting is usually a conscious mental activity, based on your rational thoughts and your present and past experience, as well as your hopes and fears. Visioning, on the other hand, gives you a sense of the future from the point of view of what I would call your wisdom self, while still keeping you connected to the real world and practical considerations.

When you set a goal in the usual way, you are describing a destination that your conscious mind believes is good for you. These beliefs may not be up-to-date or relevant to the person you are right now and, even more to the point, the person you can become.

For example, some goals, if you look closely, may turn out to be your parents' unachieved dreams, so in a sense you are doing it for them without necessarily knowing it. This is actually very common. Perhaps your mother never got an education, so you had to. Some goals may have emerged from decisions you have taken in the past that created an investment that you don't want to give up on. Maybe that education cost a lot of time and money so you can't afford to throw it all away. Some goals are simply a direct line from where you are to where you want to be. Perhaps you feel insecure financially so all you can think of is that you need to find a secure job and stick to it.

None of these goals takes account of the possibility that what you really want is around a corner, and not on a straight line at all. None reminds you that this plan sounds and looks good but it is not what your heart desires or your soul is whispering.

This is where visioning comes in.

ENERGY FOLLOWS THOUGHT

There is an ancient spiritual saying that energy follows thought. What this means is that once you see something in your inner eye, your energy flows towards creating that.

Your energy doesn't distinguish the negative fear-based thoughts from the positive inspiration-based ones. So, as they say, be careful what you wish for, and indeed what you think.

I remember the year I just had too many names to remember: I was lecturing to huge classes at college, facilitating big personal development groups, and welcoming large numbers of participants to our Skyros holidays[1]. I was pretty good at remembering names, but I just got sick of it. I said to myself petulantly, 'I'm not going to learn any more names.' And from that day on, I lost my aptitude for learning names. It was not that I couldn't remember any, but it took three times as much effort as before.

As I was quite young at the time, I cannot put it all down to ageing. And indeed, that is not the only time I promised myself something a bit silly in a petulant or frustrated mood, and then had to deal with the effects for years to come.

This is why it is so important to use your inner imagery to tap into your deepest intuition about what is really right for you, rather than to think you want things that you don't really, truly want. To do this, you need to be willing to surrender any conscious plans of your own, and just see what messages come to you from your wisest self. Then what you see in your inner eye will become a blueprint to follow in the outer world.

It has become almost a regular occurrence for someone to recognize me in a public place, anywhere in the world, and thank me for a visioning exercise they had done with me years before. So many of them had seen a future they wanted, changed course in life completely – and were really happy they had.

Just as I was proofreading this chapter, I passed by a large billboard with this quote by Albert Einstein, 'Imagination is everything. It is the preview of life's coming attractions.'

Mind, heart and soul

One very simple way to look at the difference between what you *think* you want and what you truly want is to focus on your mind, your heart and your soul and ask them what each wants. In general, the control mind talks of what you think you should do, the heart talks of your passion and what you love, and the soul talks of your truth. You have already done variations of this conversation in other chapters.

◆

Try this: First, focus on your forehead, where the thoughts of your 'control mind' live, and ask it what it wants. Then say, 'My mind says'… and finish the sentence. When you do this, be careful not to predict the answer. Just say, 'My mind says' and wait till something comes up.

Making sense of the future with this part of the mind is rational, sensible and on a straight line from now to then, but it doesn't take account of the bigger picture of the whole person.

Now, to find out what you want on a deeper level, focus on your heart, and ask it what it wants. Then say 'My heart says'… and wait for the answer. This should give you some idea of your heart's desire.

Now try talking to the soul, whatever this might

mean to you. Imagine a big light behind you, and we'll call that the soul. Now focus on this light, and ask what it wants. 'My soul says'… and again, wait for what comes up.

Does this give you a larger truth?

Which answer works best for you right now? Or do they all make sense on different levels?

SOUL TIME

There is another step we can take to find what we want, which is to step into timelessness, or, as I like to call it 'soul time'. In the dimension of timelessness, you can experience your future as if it were here right now, because, on that level, it is.

You may not believe in a dimension where sequential time disappears, and where past, present and future are as one, but your imagination does. So let your imagination do its thing and be a vehicle for your deepest sense of who you are and *then* decide whether it works for you.

The most vivid way I have found to do visioning is to choose how far into the future you want to go (e.g. one year or five years or when you are 80), and what kind of future you want to see (e.g. one in which you are happy in your life) and then imagine you are in a time-and-space ship and can go there. This is the visioning exercise in the Spiritual Gym at the end of this chapter.

First you go off the face of the Earth into a dimension where past, present and future are one, beyond the tyranny of time, and hang out there for a few moments. This is a way to free yourself from your normal assumptions about time and space. Then you turn the time-and-space ship towards Earth again, but to that time in the future you asked to see, and you go there and fully experience it. Then, once you've experienced the future as if it is happening now, you can look back and see how you got there.

The major principle of visioning is that, instead of looking forward to see where you want to go and how to get there, which engages your rational mind, you set your intention and then jump to the future, experience it fully, and look back to see what steps you took or what attitude you changed in order to have that future.

We all know the power of hindsight. The beautiful thing about visioning is that you can get hindsight before you even start.

When you look back it is important not to do it with your rational mind, figuring out how you must have got there, or, even worse, saying that you got there in a time-and-space ship. Instead you need to let yourself actually feel as if you are in the future time using your memory to remember how you arrived at that future. If you are saying something like, 'I probably did this and that,' then you are not fully in the experience.

Is this like a crystal ball showing you psychically what the future will be? No, although in my experience, people do sometimes see something that actually happens later in exact detail, a bit like a prophetic dream. Usually, it simply gives you the best picture available to you right now of the life that is right for you.

You are engaging your intuition and getting a holistic

picture that takes account of everything you know or sense at present. Of course, when your life changes, new visions of the future may become available, a bit like getting to another corner and being able to see around that. I've seen my future as an 80-year-old many times, and each time it is a bit different, because I am already a bit different than I was.

Two futures are better than one

As in Suzy's story, I almost always do visioning with two futures, one in which you honour your truest self, and one in which you betray or abandon or neglect that truest self. In other words, you might go five years forward to a positive future, and also five years forward to an unhappy future, and see the difference.

Why not just a positive future? It would be a bit like walking with your nose in the air and not looking down to see the puddles. By doing two futures, you can really see what you do and don't want, and how easy it is to get a future you don't want unless you really focus. Suzy's experience is a graphic example of learning how to avoid your normal pitfalls and take a positive way forward.

Think of it like trying on clothes in a shop. When you've seen yourself in two very different coats, you'll have a better idea about which one you want to buy, if any. I always say, when people are imagining the negative future and feeling a bit shocked or upset, 'You've seen it. You don't have to have it.'

It can be very life-affirming to see and know that you have a choice and what your choices are. When you see the negative future, it will not be one that you find difficult to imagine, or even to believe in. This is because it really is one of your possibilities. Why else would you end up in negative situations more times than can be accounted for by chance alone?

When working in a group, I get people to compete in little groups as to who has the worst negative future! We laugh in order not to cry, as they say.

You also become very conscious of what it takes for you to have a future that you could be happy with, and what it takes for you to slide your way into an unhappy one. I say 'slide into' because, as you may remember, the number one thing people say about getting to their negative future is that they just have to keep doing what they're doing.

When I ask people which future they want, the miserable one or the good one, they laugh. But the truth is that although very few people I have worked with actually decide to go for the unhappy one, most people can recognize that there is a leaning in them towards it and that they have to counteract it in order to choose the positive one.

Why? It's safe, it's secure, it's familiar, you won't have to change anything, and there's no risk. Of course, having a negative future turns out to be none of these things, but it may not feel like that at the outset.

I'll never forget the woman who actually chose the negative future because, 'I can't bring my mother into the positive future.'

We all laughed, but we also knew it was quite serious. Of course, if this was how she was seeing things, she needed to do something about her relationship with her mother so she could have the positive future with her mother in the picture.

If you find you want to go for the negative one, just acknowledge that there is no new beginning for you right now, and see how that feels. You may want to change your mind.

If you really do continue to choose the negative one, at least you will know it was a choice, and when you get there, you will have nothing to moan about, and in fact can congratulate yourself on your success at achieving the future that is making you unhappy!

Whichever you choose, it is important to send back messages to the present you, including writing a letter, telling the present you what you need to be aware of. This helps you not to lose all the wisdom you have gained when you get back to everyday life and to become really clear about what you need to know in order to have a future that you want.

How do I know this is not just wish fulfilment?

Visioning only works if you are truly open to what may be, rather than knowing what you want consciously, and trying to make the vision show that.

How do you know when it is an authentic, free image from your imagination and when it is just wish fulfilment? You may not at first. It takes time to learn to distinguish the two, between that sense that they are coming through to you from some other part of you, and the feeling that the images that come up are under your control and not surprising.

Authentic images tend to have a feeling of both familiarity and surprise about them. As one of my students put it, it's what you know but haven't told yourself. If what comes up is exactly what you thought consciously, and you are not learning anything new, then you are probably not having an authentic and illuminating image from your wisdom self.

Your motivation is very important here. If you feel you absolutely have to have one particular future or life is not worth living, you won't be able to get to your real images. You need to surrender, and ask to be shown the truth, not the story you want to hear.

I remember one woman who absolutely wanted to see a boyfriend in her future. Every time she tried to do a visioning, she just couldn't be open to her imagination, because she was desperately trying to steer her images in the direction she wanted.

I had another student who feared that the positive future she was going to see would not include her husband. But she was willing to surrender and find out the truth. She discovered to her great relief that he was right there in her positive future, adding to her joy.

Sometimes, also, the images are so unrealistic and unbelievable that you begin to guess that this might be your wish fulfilment. Authentic images have a grounded feeling about them – they are not usually your favourite fantasy writ large. That said, they may show you a future that is beyond your own sense of what is possible, and if they do, just smile and say thank you.

Ultimately, you need to ask yourself, 'Am I willing to put truth first, even if it is not what I want to see?' If you are, you are going to be able to truly tap into your authentic creative imagination.

AND NOW FOR SOMETHING COMPLETELY DIFFERENT

As with all imagery work, don't judge your vision as you are going along. Draw your conclusions later. Remember that this is an adventure and, if you can, enjoy even the scary or hair-raising or painful bits. All will have something to offer you.

For now, all you need is your curiosity and your willingness to wander in the world of the imagination and discover whatever you discover. Later you will find yourself able to take charge of your life with a new sense of authority about what is possible and how you can make it happen. You will have authority because you will know it from direct experience.

Difficult as it is to grasp this with your rational mind, in the world of the imagination – which is also a real world albeit a different one than everyday reality – when you put yourself into the future rather than just looking forward, you really are time-travelling, you really are going into the future, and it really can change your life.

Your Spiritual Gym
Exercise 7:
Visioning Your Possible Futures

Materials needed: Imagework Diary and pen and paper.

Before you do this exercise, please go back and reread the 8 Tips to Harnessing Your Imagination on page 42. This is a longer exercise than usual, and it is a particularly good exercise to do with a buddy, taking turns to read the exercise to each other. You can also buy a CD or download an MP3 that takes you, or both of you, through it (http://www.dinaglouberman.com/shop/#cd-list). Either way, it will leave you free to relax and be guided.

In this exercise, I help you create an image of a time-and-space ship, which you must see, feel, sense, smell and know. The more vivid it is, the more it will take you solidly out of everyday reality and into the world of the imagination. Remember that vivid isn't always visual. Your strongest senses may be feeling or touch or smell or sound. As long as you feel you are really there, and can suspend everyday reality for a little while, you are on your way.

This exercise can be used with respect to any time period in the future at all. If you want very specific answers about something, it helps to do a shorter time period, but not less than six months. When you choose a longer time period, say when you are 80 years old, you are getting a sense of your life values, and also dealing with issues about ageing. I love doing the 80-year-old one, and even a 90-year-old one, and they can be quite transformative.

Before you start, decide on the time period that you want to explore in terms of what age you will be, or how many years from now.

1. Relax: Choose any method you like or one of those I've outlined in previous Spiritual Gyms that worked well for you. Here's one you've done before:

   a. Breathe ten breaths, leaving a space after each outbreath and inbreath. Roll your eyeballs up, hold them and let them drop.

   b. Focus on your whole body and say, 'My whole body, relax, deeply relax, completely relax.' Now focus on each body part in turn and say, 'The crown of my head, relax, deeply relax, completely relax' and so on through your body. Notice particularly relaxing your eyelids, letting your jaw drop, relaxing your shoulders and your spine. Then focus on your mind: 'My mind, relax, deeply relax, completely relax.' Then on your emotions: 'My emotions, relax, deeply relax, completely relax.'

   c. Now imagine you are bringing down a big ball of light from above you pulling it through your body, and everywhere it touches it relaxes, softens, brings peace, and absorbs whatever doesn't benefit you, finally rolling through your heels into the earth, depositing it all into the earth to be transformed. Then invite a feeling of lightness from the earth through your feet, your torso, your neck and your head, and release it as if through a hole in the top of your head.

d. Say to yourself, 'Now surrender.'

2. Imagine you're in a time-and-space ship that can travel through space and through time, going off the face of the Earth. What is your time-and-space ship like? Imagine you are sitting on a plush seat, and you are seeing these controls:

   a. A dial to set the time you are going to. You can do this in terms of how many years forward it is, or what the date will be, or what age you will be, whichever makes easiest intuitive sense to you.

   b. A lever to put UP if you are going to the future period feeling good about your life because you have honoured your true self, or DOWN if you are going to the same time in the future but feeling bad about your life because you have neglected or betrayed your true self.

   c. A Go button.

Set the time dial, and put the lever DOWN so you can go to the negative future first and get it over with. Do it all physically, using your hands to make the movements.

3. Once you can feel the seat and have set the controls,

press the Go button, and imagine going off the face of the Earth, the Earth becoming smaller and smaller, to a dimension where past, present and future are one, beyond the tyranny of time. Rest there for a while. How is it?

4. Now point your time-and-space ship towards Earth. Press your Go button. Go towards Earth to that time in the future you've set on your dial, feeling *bad* about your life because you haven't honoured your true self. The Earth is getting larger and larger and you land. Spend a moment in the ship, and then get out and look around. Notice what you can see, what you are wearing and how you feel.

5. Now ask yourself, 'What is my bad feeling?' This doesn't mean what is the feeling about, but what actually is the feeling itself? Once you've got the feeling, ask, 'What's at the heart of this feeling? What do I feel bad about?' Now look back at your life since you set out on this visioning journey and ask: 'What is the most important thing I did to make that happen?' Look specifically at your relationships with others, your work or creativity, your relationship with yourself, and your attitude to life and death. What do you notice about each of these? How did you get yourself here?

6. If you could send a message back to the person you were when you set out on this journey, whom we will call Present Self, telling them the recipe for ending up feeling as bad as you do, what would you say? (e.g.

'Don't believe in yourself' or 'Don't take risks'). If you're with a buddy, you could compete as to whose negative future is worse! That makes it more humorous and less tragic, which usually helps. Remember to tell yourself, 'I've seen it, and I don't have to have it.'

7. When you've seen as much as you need to, and have sent your message to Present Self, get back in your time-and-space ship, press that Go button, and get out of there! Go back to your resting place outside space and time. Imagine washing yourself in a 'decontamination shower' to get rid of all those thoughts, pictures and attitudes from that negative period. Reflect on what you have learned.

8. Now point the time-and-space ship back towards Earth, put the lever UP, so you can see that time in the future feeling good about your life, and press the Go button. Go towards Earth at that time in the future, feeling great about your life. The Earth is getting larger and larger and finally you land. Spend a moment in the ship, and then get out and look around. Notice how you feel and what you are wearing. What's different?

9. Now ask yourself, 'What is my good feeling? What's at the heart of it? What do I feel best about?' Now look back and ask, 'What is the most important thing I did to make that happen?' Now begin to look specifically at your relationships with others, your work or creativity, your relationship with yourself, and your attitude to life and death. How are they different from the first future?

The more specific you can be, the more of a guide it will be to what is your best way forward. Take your time over this bit to get it as clear as you possibly can. What work are you doing exactly? Who is in your life? What do you do to take care of yourself? That sort of thing. And how is this different from in the first future?

10. The big question now is what you did differently to get to this future rather than the other one. What were the steps you took or the attitude shift you had to get here? How were they different from the first future? Be as specific as possible.

11. Now take a piece of paper, or a page in your Imagework diary, and write a letter from the future to the present. Put the future date at the top, and write Dear (your name) 20XX (the present year). Now write to the Present Self, being as specific as possible, telling them what they need to know to get where they are going. The more specific, the better: Just saying 'be yourself at all times' probably won't be all that much help. Sign it Love, (your name) (future date). For example, put May 2023 at the top, write to Dear Alice 2013, and sign off Love from Alice 2023. It's particularly wonderful to put this letter in an envelope, and have someone else address it, so that you don't recognize the handwriting, and then post it to you. You'll see how good this is when you get it and don't know whom it's from until you open it.

12. Now press the Go button, go off the face of the Earth,

back to your dimension where past, present and future are one, and spend some time reflecting on both futures and what you've learned.

13. Keeping the lever UP, set the dial to the present time, press the Go button, and go back to the present, feeling good about your life. You land, get out of your time-and-space ship and come back into your body in the room. What is good about your life right now?

14. Can you recognize the part of you that wants the first future, and the part of you that wants the second future? Which future do you choose? Are you willing to do what you have to do to get there even if it is daunting? What do you need to do?

15. Thank the future you for his or her help and ask them to serve as an adviser for you when you need them. How will you specifically and practically carry through these understandings?

16. Use your Imagework Diary to record the experience as fully as possible and to make some commitments to yourself about getting to the future you have chosen. We will talk more about making the choice, saying *Yes* and committing to it in the coming chapter.

17. If you are still feeling a bit in a trance, count yourself up or have your buddy count you up: 'I'm going to count up from 1–5 and when I say 5 I'm going to open my eyes (you're going to open your eyes), relaxed and alert,

bringing the peace and wisdom back with me (with you). 1–2-eyelids lightening, 3-4-coming to the surface, 5. Eyes open. I stamp my feet (stamp your feet) and come back to the room.' Three stamps.

QUICK VISIONING

This brief format is particularly useful if you are doing this exercise regularly or for short-term goals and decisions which can be a matter of hours or up to six months:

1. It's X time from now (or: It's the end of this event) and I feel good about it. What is the good feeling? What did I do to bring that about?

2. It's X time from now (or: It's the end of this event) and I feel awful about it. What is the awful feeling? What did I do to bring it about?

3. Which do I want? Am I willing to go for it and do what I have to do to get there?

4. You can finish with the bubble exercise you will find in Spiritual Gym Exercise 8, step 11 on page 168.

STEP THREE:

YOUR NEW BEGINNING

CHAPTER 8

Saying Yes

You now have a vision of two possible futures, you've looked back to see how you got to each, and hopefully you've chosen the one you want to go for. This vision is a map that can guide you towards your new beginning.

But the map is not the territory. How do you actually make it happen in the world of everyday reality?

As always, the first thing is to say *Yes*. In this case, it is a whole-hearted *Yes* to this vision and to all that is involved in getting there, a *Yes* that engages all of your being, not just your head. Chad Varah, whose story is in Chapter 1, did this when he took his vow. Robert Bly talks similarly in my interview with him, below, of a decision he made not to shame his children.

Sometimes it takes time to get to a *Yes*. One of my students, when I remarked to him, 'That must have been hard to say,' answered, 'It was easy to say it, but it was hard to get to the place where it was easy.' The same can go for getting to a *Yes*. Shakti Gawain, author of the groundbreaking book *Creative Visualization*, talks below of this process of getting to the place where a *Yes* was easy.

Once you have said the *Yes*, the rest follows. You still need compassion, respect, focus, discipline, persistence, hard work, more hard work and a lot more, but you have set your course and you are committed to it, and that makes all the difference.

ROBERT BLY'S STORY

Robert Bly, author of the profoundly influential book *Iron John*[1], poet and leader of a worldwide men's movement, told me this story about the moment he made a whole-hearted commitment to his new path.

> *The turning point that moved me into this work had to do with my children... I began to recognize, as someone who came out of Norwegian Lutherans, how much shame I passed onto my children. I had shame in my childhood and I was passing it on by shaming them.*
>
> *I invented the word 'shame tanks'. When we are small our shame tanks get very full, and we have to pass it onto someone else. In the playground probably. And now I am an adult my shame tanks are still full from childhood. Who do you empty them on? Your children.*
>
> *So I made a decision – I'm not going to shame them anymore. That's it.*
>
> *I could feel the change in them immediately. And I feel less ashamed myself. The most ashamed thing is after you have shamed someone.*[2]

SHAKTI GAWAIN'S STORY

Robert Bly didn't say how long it took him to get to his decision. Shakti Gawain talked of a ten-year process from visualizing a good relationship with a man and finding her partner.

As the author of *Creative Visualization*,[3] the book that catapulted the concept of visualization into the public understanding in 1978, Shakti Gawain has often been associated with the idea that if you visualize something powerfully enough it will happen. But when I interviewed her in the early 1990s, it was fascinating to discover that her view had evolved and she did not consider the process to be quite so straightforward. She now believed that visualizing something may actually be just the beginning of a process of getting to a *Yes*.

Shakti Gawain's *Yes* didn't come as a statement of commitment or decision or vow as for Chad Varah and Robert Bly, but as an intuition that emerged after a deep healing that brought her home to herself.

My most difficult area was personal relationships with men. It took me about ten years from the time I started visualizing the man I wanted to actually find a relationship. Often by asking for what you want, you invite the healing process that you need to go through in order to have it.

A key moment in my healing process was when I realized there was a part of me that didn't want a relationship. Often when we think we want something and it's not happening, there's a part of us that is blocking it and for good reason. I discovered I had a lot of fear of losing my freedom, of losing my focus in my work, and of giving myself away too much.

After finishing my third book, Return to the Garden, I felt I had completed a certain level of healing in my life. I was able to be with myself, to be with my own vulnerability. At that point I knew intuitively that the right relationship would come along. It had happened inside and it was going to get reflected! Within three weeks of that moment, I connected with Jim, my husband. We got together and it was an instant 'Oh gosh, here he is.'[4]

I WOULD LOVE MYSELF UNCONDITIONALLY IF ONLY I WERE DIFFERENT

Shakti Gawain was able to open to a relationship when she could value herself, be with herself, live with her own vulnerability, and, I guess, though she doesn't say it explicitly, honour her own achievement in publishing her third book. In other words, she had to feel she was okay just as she was, and that she had the strength to hold onto her own focus and direction whether or not she had a partner.

Only then could she safely invite someone else into her life, knowing she would not lose herself. As soon as she was good with herself, her heart and soul whispered that she could have the relationship she had always wanted, and so she did.

You need to be pulled towards the future by the power of your inspiration and your vision, by those heart and soul whispers, not pushed by your need to be loveable or of value. Creating a better life for yourself is definitely not about proving that you are an okay person, worthy of love and respect. You are already an okay person, worthy of love and respect. This is what unconditional love is all about, and is absolutely essential, especially when you are trying to change something about yourself and your life.

I once wrote an article called 'I would love myself unconditionally if only I were different'.[5] That just about sums up the heart of the challenge – and the unspoken contracts we make with ourselves – in any work we do on new beginnings. So often when we talk of unconditional self-love, we secretly believe that if we don't change, we won't really and truly be worthy of love.

The trouble is that if you send yourself, or the child in you, the message that you will only be okay if you change, it simply won't work. You will find yourself balking and not doing the work to change, because no one does their best under a barrage of criticism, or you will get where you want to go and still feel the same way about yourself.

If you were trying to help someone else make changes in their life, you would find it works exactly the same way. You'd have to accept them exactly as they are, respect their wonderful qualities and inspire them to change. It's that compassion for their limitations and respect for their magnificence we have spoken of in Chapter 5 (see page 98) that really works. Doing it by criticizing doesn't exactly float most people's boat.

Do you fear that if you accept yourself as you are, you will get stuck and never change? The opposite is true. If you don't accept yourself, you are well and truly stuck, because the most important thing about a new beginning is that you honour the person who is having that new beginning, and love them enough to want them to have it.

Remember that honouring and loving yourself does not mean that you approve of everything that you do. You may be awful at staying focused on your task, and need to work on it, but you are still loveable and magnificent.

The one has nothing to do with the other.

I know I keep going on about accepting and respecting yourself. Forgive me if I have started to sound repetitive. Maybe it's because in my years of teaching, therapy, group work, community building and coaching, I have time and again been blown away by the power and persistence of that far too common view that you are not okay as you are.

When I was teaching classes of young social science students, I used to ask them, 'How many of you believe that everyone else is okay but you?' The forest of hands that went up said it all. And remember, these were not clients or patients but just ordinary students who did not think they had a particular problem.

And there I was, a therapist and teacher, who knew first hand that this couldn't be true, because I'd been let so deeply into the lives of others and particularly into their pain. Yet I was aware of how that view often whispered its dangerous message to me in my own life.

And once, when I was running a training group in Imagework, I said these two words, 'You matter.' A shudder went through the room, and I mean this literally. I needed to repeat it a few times before it even began to sink in. It was as if it had never occurred to them.

So to get to a real *Yes* for the future, you need to check that you are doing it for the right reasons, because otherwise the whole process can hurt you rather than support you. If you get this right in your imagination, the rest will usually follow.

JACK'S STORY

Jack's desire for a new project is a good example of all this. He had set up a successful business with his wife, sold it, then started another one, which was also successful. Now that his project didn't require all his energy, and his children were about to leave home, he was looking for a new challenge. Could I help him to find the next step and take it? In other words there was a turning point ahead, and a few signs would help, as well as maybe a cheering coach to encourage him to do it.

That seemed simple enough, and I prepared to discuss with him what he really wanted and to use a few imagery techniques to help him see his next step and to take it. But then he revealed to me another piece of the puzzle. Although all the plans he had made had worked out incredibly well, including a rather wonderful marriage and two successful businesses, he was always uneasy, always felt he might be found out to be a fraud, and often had anxiety dreams.

All in all, he was pretty frightened, doubtful about himself and sometimes depressed. That was not likely to change, except temporarily, if he found himself a new project, even if, as was likely, he was successful.

It became clear to both of us that finding a new project would quiet his anxieties for a while, but would not do anything for the underlying self-doubt. A much more worthwhile goal was to find out who he really was and what he really wanted, and to begin to love and honour himself whatever he accomplished and whatever happened. Once he'd done that, any project he chose would be just fine.

The same is true for you.

YES TO NOW AND YES TO CHANGE

In order to facilitate this process of an authentic *Yes*, it is good to think of it as saying *Yes* to where you are now as well as *Yes* to where you want to go. This supports the understanding that change and lovability are not connected to each other.

When I'm working with change, I like to use an image of a magic cinema, which shows you films of how you are and how you will be. The Spiritual Gym at the end of this chapter will take you through this exercise. But for the time being, follow the logic of it, and then you can do it fully and with understanding later.

You will imagine sitting in your own private cinema seeing a film of yourself as you are now, before you've made that change. Often the film is a humorous caricature of you. You may also step into the picture briefly and remind yourself exactly what it feels like.

Then the real question is: how do you feel about that person on the screen? If you love and appreciate and respect them, that's great. But if you feel sorry for them, contemptuous, dismissive, sick at the sight of them, that sort of thing, recognize that change will not do you any good.

Go back to Chapter 5 (see page 98) to check out that look that combines compassion for your limitations and respect for your magnificence. You need to send your love, which includes both compassion and respect, until the person on the screen really gets it, feels it. If they do, you'll see a change in them on the screen.

Then you know you can take that movie off the screen, into the past, and then ask that lovely person on the screen to sit next to you, and invite a movie of the future you, after you've made the change.

Why is it so important to invite a picture of how you will be after you have changed? This is because the thing that stops you often is the fact that you cannot imagine being the kind of person who achieves that goal, or that you are secretly feeling that you don't really want to achieve that goal anyway.

A little saying from my childhood always comes to mind when I think about how impossible it is to want to change if you can't imagine being that person, or think you won't like being that person. It goes: *I hate spinach but I'm glad I hate spinach because if I liked it I would eat it and I hate spinach.*

The same goes for any change you want to embark on. The more work you do to make it both possible and positive in your imagination, the less resistance you will have, and the more power you can lend the process.

If you find when you step into the picture that you don't actually like being the person on the screen, then that tells you why you haven't managed to do this before. Shakti Gawain, for example, had an unconsciously negative picture of having a relationship, believing it would stop her from feeling free and from focusing on her own development. So ask your imagination to show you a movie that you could accept, perhaps of an intermediate or smaller goal, or of a slightly revised goal.

One of my students on a Life Changes course wanted to be well organized. But once he saw the movie and stepped into it, he hated it. Why? He felt like a robot. He needed a picture of being organized that took account of his idiosyncrasies, and was comfortable for him. When he had this, he was able to say *Yes*.

If you are feeling blocked in your *Yes* and don't know why or how to overcome it, try the Spiritual Gym Exercise 1: *Where Am I and Where Do I Want to Be?* (see page 27), or Exercise 3: *Image as Life Metaphor* (see page 64) to see if you can understand what the blockage is and what you need to get past it.

When I do this exercise in a group, it is normally quite straightforward for people to choose a goal and work with it. But when I was doing my workshop on Turning Points and New Beginnings recently, the process of setting goals for this exercise included the understanding that the participants were not just choosing a goal, but that it was one that they were committing to take forward and work with seriously for the next few months. This time, the goal-setting raised all the emotional issues that people had lurking in the background. It was only when people honoured the bit of their emotional history that had been getting in their way that they could go on to find serious goal-setting possible. It was another case of it being difficult to get to the place where it was easy! So don't be surprised if feelings come up that you are not expecting and that are asking to be dealt with before you can move on.

Once you've decided you do want this future you that you have seen, you can move to the process of committing to it, intending and releasing, and getting going.

YOUR INNER EXPERTS

When you are working with the Magic Cinema exercise, below, you will find that at some point in the exercise you turn around and see someone who is an expert in what you are trying to do. You ask the expert for help, and you switch roles and become the expert, and respond. Somehow, when you are being the expert, you will know things you didn't know you knew. This is part of the power of imagery.

Conversations with an inner expert can become a normal part of your daily life. If there is anyone you feel might be able to do what you can't do, or knows something you want to know, make it a point to imagine them clearly, talk to them, ask them what you want to ask, and switch roles and respond. Then switch back to being yourself and receive the message. You can do this also with wise spiritual beings, or a boss you don't understand, or a historical figure you admire. You can even talk directly to trees, or statues in a museum, or even rubbish bins, ask them questions and sense their response. Yes, even rubbish bins may have a point of view you may need to listen to!

If all this sounds a bit mad and unbelievable, please try it and see. You will find that you are gaining access to a wider range of points of view and understandings than you ever thought possible. Why limit yourself to people that you meet face-to-face in everyday life when the imagination is so full of other wonderful possibilities?

INTENDING AND RELEASING

Paradoxically, you can only get to a powerful and authentic *Yes* if you don't need to succeed at what you are intending to do. My friend Sara is an outstanding therapist and trainer with a wonderful writing talent, and has a book she wants to write that could be very important for a lot of people. But she never gets around to writing it.

When I enquired further, I discovered that she was afraid of publishing the book and being told it wasn't much good.

I suggested to her that all she had to set as her intention was to write the book and finish it, and that she wasn't guaranteeing to anyone or to herself that she would write a great book or a successful book or a book that was critically acclaimed. This freed her from her ambivalence, and then and there she set her intention to write the book. I very much look forward to reading it.

When you set an intention to do something, and you follow through, that in itself is a great achievement. On the level of self esteem, i.e. how good you feel about yourself, the process of deciding to do something, doing it, and completing it is wonderful. It gives you a confidence in your own will, and in your own ability to do what you say you will do. This is crucial to building a well-integrating, highly functioning personality.

It also works on the level of soul esteem, which we talked of in Chapter 5 (see page 97), which is about being willing to honour the whisperings of your heart and soul and follow them without counting the cost or even having the self esteem to believe you are good enough. If you are inspired to do something, and you do it, it is as if you support your heart and soul's purpose in life, and know on a deep level that you are willing to align yourself with your highest and your best.

But all you need to build both self esteem and soul esteem is to show willing, to put your will behind the commitment, not be swayed by feelings that may vary, and do what you said you would do.

You do not actually need to succeed. That is not fully up to you.

Do you make the unspoken assumption that if you take a risk, it must succeed or you have failed? Many people do. But a risk is a risk. It has a good chance, yes, but it can go wrong. No blame.

So when you are choosing to do whatever you have to in order to get there, you also need to surrender to whatever you don't have control over, which can include your own unconscious, luck, fate, universal will, or whatever you believe in. You are not omnipotent. You can't make it happen and, though it is likely, it is never certain. You also don't have to have it. In the unlikely event that it doesn't work out, you will still be okay.

You are powerful beyond your wildest dreams, but you are *never* all-powerful.

When I help people commit themselves to their vision, I always say that they need to 'intend and release.'

As you will see in Step 11 of the Spiritual Gym exercise in this chapter, you put an image of yourself having achieved your goal in a bubble, and say, 'I ask and intend for this to be.' This means that you will do whatever you have to do to achieve your goal, and you are asking for the help of your own unconscious, other people, the universe, and indeed anything or anyone you trust, to support you.

But then you also say, 'And I release it.' This means that you cannot *make* it happen, though you can do your very best, and, moreover, you don't *have* to have it. The farmer can till the soil and plant the crops and tend to them, but can't make the sun shine or the rain fall. If it doesn't work out, and you have done your best, you will still be okay and be able to ask what's next.

Only then can you say a full *Yes*, send the bubble out into the domain of potential waiting to be actualized, and let your will go to work to make it happen.

Try this: *The success coach Raymond Aaron[6] has this way of helping people with goals that they are procrastinating about: You set yourself three goals – Minimum, Target and Outrageous. Minimum is the least you are willing to commit to (I'll just do one hour practising my horn to see how I get on). Target is actually your goal (I will learn this jazz piece). Outrageous is what you could hardly dream of doing (I will set up a gig to perform it).*

Try this method for fun, and you may find it very powerful. This is because you are visualizing three powerful possibilities, and visualizing brings it into the realm of potential, and yet you only demand of yourself to do the least of them. Sometimes once you get started on the minimum, and in this way overcome your procrastination and ambivalence, you just can't stop yourself from Target or even Outrageous.

BEYOND YOUR PERSONAL SELF

When your heart and soul whisper, it's never only about you, but about the nature of being human, and your place in the world, and the part you play. This is what soul esteem is all about.

It does help if whatever it is you are aiming for has a sense about it that it is not only good for you, but also for others. Of course, when you are happier, everyone feels better around you. And if what you are doing is in your highest best interest, it will be in the highest best interest of everyone around.

But there is also this: if you believe that what you are aiming for will benefit others as well as yourself, you are more likely to do it and less likely to give up on it. You will also feel better about yourself, and better about others.

Robert Bly (see page 149) talked about how when he decided to give up shaming his children, they immediately felt better, but he himself also felt less ashamed. Similarly Loraine (see page 73) gave up on revenge partly because she didn't want to perpetuate the cycle of violence in the world, and the upshot of her struggle was to come to the beginnings of peace for herself as well as to take a course that will enable her to benefit others. We are, after all, interconnected.

Besides this, if every new beginning were for others as well as yourself, you would be contributing to the ripple effect of positive transformation in the world.

And this, as you may have already guessed, is the deep commitment that is at the heart of my writing this book.

Your Spiritual Gym
Exercise 8:
The Magic Cinema

Materials needed: Your Imagework Diary, oil pastels or crayons.

Start this exercise by thinking back to your visioning of your positive future, and choosing one important aspect that you want to focus on now. It should be something that you know you want, but you find difficult. Decide exactly what you want to go for – what change in yourself, creative project or new beginning. Say, aloud if possible, 'I want to xxxx', being as specific as possible.

Ask yourself if you would really go for it if it were on offer. If so, say out loud, 'I choose to be/do/achieve/have… and fill in whatever is in that picture. The word 'choose' is very important. It is also important to say clearly exactly what it is you are choosing.[7] Say this as a statement of commitment in a positive, full way, but use words a five-year-old can understand, so your whole being knows how very real it is.

Now feel what happens in your body as you do the exercise. If something seems to shift in your body, then you have said a real *Yes*. If not, do it again with all your heart and body and soul.

If you find you can't say this, ask yourself what is stopping you, and what you need to get past this. Ask it as an open question to your heart or soul, and see what your heart or soul has to say. Or do a drawing of what is stopping you and another one of what you need to get past it, and add some words. That should help you to get a sense of it, and work something out.

Now, make this even stronger by doing this Magic Cinema imaging:

1. Relax: Use any technique you have enjoyed so far, or any you normally use. Or try this brief one we did in Spiritual Gym Exercise 4: Close your eyes. Roll your eyes up to the ceiling. Forget your eyes. Notice any tension in your body. Say hello to it and smile. Forget your body. Imagine a big light above your head, larger than your shoulders, and pull it slowly through your body, imagining that it heals, and softens, and cleanses and clears and absorbs anything you don't need right now. Finally, it sinks through your feet into the earth, depositing whatever it has absorbed to be transformed. Allow a lightness to come up from the ground through your whole body, and then out through the top of your head. Surrender. Let go and see what happens.

2. Imagine that you are in your own private cinema. You're sitting in the best seat in the house, watching a magic screen. Once you can feel the seat, and see or sense the screen, allow a picture of yourself to emerge on the screen as you are now, before you've made this life change. Don't be surprised if it is quite a funny caricature of yourself, or a gross exaggeration. Watch yourself as if you are an actor in a film and notice what you notice. What is the picture? How does this person operate? I will call this person Present Self.

3. Step into the picture and be Present Self. How do you stand, walk, breathe? What is your posture like? Walk around and talk to yourself and find out what you are telling yourself. Exaggerate it to help you get a sense of it.

4. Go back to your seat in the cinema and consider: how do you feel about Present Self? Are you loving and compassionate, or are you disgusted, impatient, critical or that sort of thing? Be honest about these feelings, even if they are not pretty!

   Remember that under criticism people contract and fold up. So try seeing what Present Self is doing not as an aberration or an act of stupidity, but as the positive, though limiting, choice they are making at present. Know that they are doing their best in a difficult world. Why and how do they make this choice and what are the benefits and the disadvantages?

   Look at Present Self with compassion for their limitations and pain, and respect for their magnificence. Love and accept them as the wonderful though perhaps flawed person they are. Send this love, compassion and respect like an energy flow towards Present Self until they seem to receive it, and something changes on the screen. Once their expression changes, let the picture move off the screen to the left, into the past. This is how you were, but no longer are. Invite Present Self, who is now in the past, to sit next to you in the cinema and put your arm around them.

5. Now allow a picture to emerge of you as you will be, after you have made the life change you have chosen. Again look at the person on the screen as if at an actor in a film. How is this person different from the other one, i.e. not just in a different situation, but looking and acting differently. I will call this person Future Self.

6. Now, in your imagination, walk up to the screen and step into the picture and become Future Self. What does it feel like to be this person? How do you walk, breathe? How does your heart beat? How do you respond to the world? How is it different from how Present Self was in the previous film? Really become clear exactly how you operate and what it is that makes this way of operating so successful.

    Spend a day as Future Self, noticing all the details of how you live, including how, or whether, you get up in the morning, brush your teeth, eat your breakfast, go to work, have leisure time and go to bed at night. Notice also how you deal with the things that Present Self found difficult.

7. If you don't like Future Self, or can't tolerate the anxiety of being that person, or don't get any image at all, don't despair: this just tells you why it's all been so difficult to do. Go back to your cinema seat, and play around in your mind with the image of yourself until you find one that is comfortable. Think of other people who do it well, or of how you could make that change and still be likeable, or just wonder: if I could make that change in

a way I could feel good about it, how would it be? Then ask for another image of how you will be after you've made the change that you will be happy with, and if you get one, step into that one. If it still feels threatening to be that person, you may want to try out only moments of being that person until you feel more comfortable. And even if the screen is totally empty, you can still step into it – you will probably find that a feeling emerges even though the picture wasn't there. I used to find that when people were trying to stop smoking, their image of themselves as non-smokers was often a complete blank! Many found it simply impossible to imagine it until they stepped into the picture.

8. While being the person on the screen, imagine that you now have standing behind you a helper who is an expert at what you are trying to do. This could be a real or imaginary person, someone you know personally or a historical or spiritual figure. Turn around to discover the identity of your expert. It might surprise you. Ask their name, if you don't know who they are, and what they are a specialist in. What do they say? Now ask them whatever you like about your new role. Step into their image and be them. How does it feel to be this expert? What is your essential quality or attitude? Look back at Future Self. What can you see about them that they might not know? Respond with help, support or advice. Then switch back to being Future Self again, receive that message, and consider how this can help you. Be aware that you can call on them whenever you need them in future.

9. Look back and see what led up to this point. What steps did you take? Look back at Present Self. How did you get from there to here? What shift did you make that made this possible? This bit is very important so be as specific as possible.

10. Now step out of the picture and go back to your seat. Look at that person on the screen, and recognize that this is really you as you could be and will be. Can you make a real decision that this goal is a) possible, b) desirable, c) one that you have a right to have or is right for you to have, and d) one that you are willing to put your energy and intentions behind?

11. If so, do this bubble exercise.

   a. See yourself having accomplished everything you have set out to accomplish, looking happy, proud, contented, or whatever emotion seems to come, and put this picture in a bubble.

   b. Ask yourself if you are willing to follow through consistently and do your best, and also to be open to any help from others or from the universe. Are you willing to show willing? If so, say, aloud if possible, 'I ask and intend for this to be.'

   c. Ask yourself if you can acknowledge that this is not all up to you, and that you are willing to surrender to that which goes beyond you, including your unconscious, fate, luck, the universe, God, or whatever you believe in. If so, say, aloud if possible, 'I release it.'

d. Blow the bubble out with a strong expulsive breath into the domain of potential waiting to be actualized. If you are working with a buddy, you can put both bubbles into a larger bubble, and blow it out together.

e. Stand up, and say, aloud if at all possible, with all the power you can muster, 'So must it be NOW' and during the NOW make a strong gesture with your arm and stamp your foot. This needs to have so much power that it feels as if you are commanding the universe within and without to obey. You may need to try three or four times until you feel something really transform inside you, as if the molecules are reordering themselves!

12. Appreciate yourself for this experience, reflect on the concrete implications of what you learned and look forward to seeing what you intend to do in a practical sense to make your vision come true. If the goal seems difficult or just needs more practice, spend a few moments every day practising being that person you will be after you've made this life change. Or just tell yourself you are already that person, and describe your attributes. And before you enter into a situation in which you could use that skill, or before you practise in real life, focus for a moment on being that person once again.

13. Write about it in your Imagework Diary and/or draw a picture that represents the two selves.

CHAPTER 9

I Can Do This
One Step at a Time

This chapter is about creating your new life, one step at a time, one brick at a time, with joy. When you have a purpose, a plan, compassion and respect for yourself, good connections with others, plus a determination to stay peaceful, the way there can be as joyful as the getting there.

Joy is different from happiness. It is not to do with success in the world, but with that creative life force within you and around you that just flows and gives life form and meaning.

I like to say that joy is the gift of the soul.

You might be struggling, in pain, facing difficulties, even what seem like insuperable obstacles, but if on some level you know you are doing what you choose to do, or what you feel called upon to do, there is always joy. Just stop a moment and look for the joy underneath the everyday stuff that fills your mind and blocks out the whispers of your heart and soul. It will be there, waiting for you to quiet down and connect.

CONNIE'S STORY

So how do you get going with your new beginnings? Let's start with Connie's story, to get an idea of the steps that might be involved.

Connie Ragen Green has recently created a successful career in internet marketing and training. I was delighted to interview her about how she travelled the path from difficult times to her new life. I've given a longer than usual excerpt below, because it is almost a textbook case of how all the visioning, planning, discipline, hard work, more hard work, commitment to service and leaps of faith can weave together to create a new beginning.

And then Connie has turned around, as so many inspiring people do, to help as many people as she can to do it too.

Connie's story is a reminder that the magic of new beginnings is not the abracadabra kind, but some alchemy that happens when you decide where you want to go, you honour and trust your commitment and your purpose, and you give it everything you've got and more.

I was a classroom teacher for 20 years and still did real estate, my previous profession, because teachers aren't paid much and I wanted a home and financial security.

The turning point came when I had a work injury from falling when putting up a bulletin board and at the same time I was going through cancer for a second time. I saw it was going to be too difficult to stay in the classroom. I thought there must be some other way to live than to be gone from your house 12–14 hours a day, 6–7 days a week. I left at the crack of dawn and then after school I went to real estate appointments.

I wanted a better life for me and for the people in my life that I'm connected to. I couldn't even physically continue at the pace I was going just to pay the bills. I had missed every event with my family and friends. I wanted time and financial freedom, and that, for me, meant working from home.

My prayer which I kept repeating was, 'Please God, I want to find something I can do from my bedroom, if necessary, that will allow me enough money to pay my bills with grace and ease.'

I started the journey of reading and talking to people, trying to get ideas. Day by day I took steps, did my reading, and started going to events where people were encouraged to share their dreams. At one of the events, they gave out a big book of CDs of people who had presented. I would put in about six at a time in my car and listen to one after another when I was driving.

I discovered that people were making money from websites, selling information products. In 2005, I decided that this is what I wanted to do, and within a year I also decided to leave my teaching job. I started blogging, e-marketing, producing e-books, selling information products. At first, I was just working evenings and weekends but I began earning a little.

One lecture I attended was about enrolling in a mentoring programme, and I did that. I set goals year by year, month by month and week by week. Through these programmes, I also began to connect to people who had a real desire for change.

Another turning point came in December 2005. I was living in San Fernando Valley, in the Los Angeles area, with crime and traffic getting worse all the time. One day I heard what sounded like an earthquake. A man had cut through the fence in my yard. He had been released from prison and was escaping from parole. I asked myself, 'Why am I doing this? This is insanity.'

A friend north of LA phoned and said they were building some houses. I went to see one, fell in love with the neighbourhood, and saw I could live there. I put my name down.

I moved into my new house in March 2006. I knew it would work out and I took a leap of faith. If I hadn't done the things leading up, seeking knowledge, reading books, going to events where you jump up and down, and done the mentoring programme, I wouldn't have signed up for the house. But because of the groundwork I had laid, I saw that this would be perfect for my new life.

I resigned from teaching in 2006 and gave away my real estate clients, even though at that time I wasn't earning enough to pay the bills, because I had decided that this was going to be my new life. I cashed in my pension to support myself. I thought, 'I can't wait to do this. I'd be wasting more time. I have to jump in and devote my time.'

I just sat in front of the computer, knowing I had to learn to do the business, and that I had enough money to live for about a year. I thought, 'This is what I have taken on, and I have to be willing to work very hard, and be very serious about doing it so the money lasts as long as possible.' I treated it like a job, worked 40 hours a week for my own dream, just as I had been willing to work for someone else's dream.

I was always looking for how I could serve people. At that time, I wasn't an expert and I didn't know how to create an information product. But when people were looking for information, I could be a trusted resource and offer them what I felt would serve them.

By 2008, when I really started making enough money, I saw I could do this for the rest of my life.

My life now is that I call the shots; I do what I want to do.

A typical day is this: I work from 6.30–10 am, including weekends, on work to do with my business. I'm gone from the house by 10 am, doing things in the community, different projects to do with charities. I holiday about four times a year with family and friends. I'm also travelling every month and combining work events with pleasure.

I didn't do it overnight, so when people come to me now wanting to have a business on the internet, I always ask them what their mindset is, what their desire is, how they will serve, how hard they are willing to work, and how willing they are to keep learning and keep meeting people and making connections. If they are still serious, I bring them into my courses and even then 90 per cent fall by the wayside, but

10 per cent really make it work.

Most people I meet don't want to rock the boat. They're content to live day by day. They know they won't get out of life alive and, until then, they don't want to cause problems. But I'm glad that's not me.

YOUR PURPOSE

The great theatre director Stanislavski wrote, 'There is only one thing that can lure our creative will and draw it to us, and that is an attractive aim, a creative objective... the objective gives the pulse to the living being of the role.' [1]

So now is the time to go back and look at the vision that emerged for you in the Spiritual Gym Exercise 7: *Visioning Your Possible Futures* (see page 139) This vision is the creative objective that Stanislavski was talking about.

For Connie, for example, it was encapsulated in that prayer, *Please God, I want to find something I can do from my bedroom, if necessary, that will allow me enough money to pay my bills with grace and ease.*

It is also worth reflecting on what makes this vision so important for you. Why did you say that wholehearted *Yes*? What powers the *Yes*?

For Connie, it was to do with wanting a better life for herself and for those she was connected to, and to enable her to serve others more.

What about your vision inspires *you*? What is the purpose, even the life purpose, being expressed by this vision? How central is this purpose to becoming the person you want to be and in fact truly are? On a scale from 0–10 of importance to you, how would you rate it?

Would you want this on your tombstone (whether or not you plan to have one)? What words would you want on that tombstone?

Keeping this purpose in mind can be really important when the going gets tough.

Actually it's crucial even when the going is smooth. It's what reminds you of who you are, and the real point of your new beginning.

YOUR THROUGH LINE OF ACTION

Once the inner objective is clear, you need what Stanislavski called a 'through line of action', the pattern of actions that expresses your intentions. Your plans, and your active efforts to attain your goal are your through line of action.

Remember in the visioning when you looked back and saw the steps you needed to take to get to that vision? This is your through line of action, or at least a general sketch of what it takes to get there. You will need to plan in more detail now in order to really prepare the way ahead.

Remember also that however much you plan, you need to be open to adapting your plans in the light of what emerges later, whether it is about the project, world events or your own talents and limitations. And you need to stay open to the advice of other people who have been there before you, and have a point of view that may be different to yours but may add an extra dimension to your thinking.

You will, of course, meet obstacles, circumstances and people that block you for whatever reason. According to Stanislavski, this conflict between your through line of action, and the counter through lines of actions of the world, is the thing that constitutes the drama of the play – and, of course, of life.

In other words, these obstacles are not simply frustrating blockages. They are what make your journey to a new beginning interesting, dramatic, challenging, worth getting up for in the morning.

If it were too easy, wouldn't you get bored and find something more challenging to do?

I CAN DO THIS ONE STEP AT A TIME

When you did the visioning and looked back, what steps could you see you had taken? These may not have been very specific yet, but they will at least show you the attitudes you needed to shift. To become more specific, it helps to go forward instead of backward, put in a time frame, make clear schedules, and set clear intentions to carry these out and make it all happen. Please try the Spiritual Gym Exercise, *Being Practical,* at the end of this chapter to start you off on planning your project.

Your mantra now needs to be, *I can do this one step at a time.*

David Whyte, an extraordinary poet who also works in the corporate world to unlock creativity, spoke in a lecture I attended of the decision he made to be a poet in the corporate world, a career for which there was little or no precedent. And then he described how he got from his previous career to his new one, while still working in a full-time stressful job.

He committed himself to do one thing every day that could take him closer to his goal. And so he did. Within a

177

matter of months, he had his breakthrough, when he was invited to replace a speaker who had cancelled.

He talked of how he lay on the floor in the back of the auditorium, sick to his stomach, unable to believe he would get up and speak. But then he did. And once he got going, he saw that this was his thing, and he was completely at home doing it.

Can you take one step a day towards your vision? Can you trust yourself even when you are terrified, to just keep going, and stay on course?

And without further ado, take the first step.

You're on your way.

---◆---

Try this: You may want to make your vision more real by physically experiencing what you are going for. You are going to write a book, so create the cover, or a press release, and put them up on your wall. You want to open a boutique bed-and-breakfast? Visit one that you love, find out how it looks and how it works, and then see and feel yourself running it. The more real your vision can become, the more you will know deep down inside that this is a real plan and not a pipe dream.

DAILY SCHEDULES

It is now time to create daily schedules that include not only your work commitments, but also those to do with the rest of your life. For some of you, scheduling comes easy and you do it all the time. But for those who don't find it so easy, like myself, or for the very many of you that always create a schedule for work but not for your life, here are some thoughts.

To keep yourself focused, it always helps to plan what you will be doing on any particular day, which doesn't just mean work but all of your life. How you do this is up to you. Some people like to draw up a schedule the night before, including the time you will do each of the various tasks and activities you plan. I myself prefer to get up in the morning and meditate, and then make my list.

But be aware, or should I say beware, of your own tendencies to put too much in your schedule. If you habitually don't get everything done, and end up feeling bad, it may well be that it's not you that's in the wrong, but the plan.

If you like David Whyte's approach of doing one thing a day towards your goal, add that one thing to your daily schedule and give it special star value. This means that you must make sure it gets done, and doesn't just get moved aside because of all the 'urgent' tasks.

Or you may feel that you want to set a whole day aside for certain kinds of tasks. Many people prefer to set aside whole days for their creative and developmental tasks, and to confine other 'maintenance' or admin jobs to other days.

For example, when I am writing, I try to set aside clear days until say 3 or 4 pm and, where possible, I do it in my retreat flat in Hastings, away from the rough and tumble of London life. Then I try to keep writing days as writing days, admin days as admin days, and I try to make appointments with clients in the late afternoon. When I do admin on my writing days, which can't be avoided sometimes, I keep it to the absolute minimum.

And while you are at it, what is your free day? Here I have a strong view that you should have one free day a week that is yours to do what you like with. You may remember how in Chapter 4 (see page 78) I talked about Shabbat as the day when you do things only for the present and not for the future?

Can you give yourself one Shabbat day a week? Or failing that, half a day? Or failing that, two days? Try scheduling it in, and find out whether you get more or less done in the long run.

And for that matter, have you scheduled in your holidays? Be generous with these; this is your life, after all, and why shouldn't you enjoy it 100 per cent?

Besides, working without any holidays is a bit like selling off the family silver – in the end, you realize that the gains were short term.

Remember also the principle of carrot rather than stick. At the end of the day, and at the end of each week, congratulate yourself on what you have accomplished. At the end of every goal accomplished, whether small or big, do the same. And focus on anything that didn't go as well as you hoped as a learning experience that you can gain from, rather than as fodder for self attack.

Try this: *At the end of your working day, congratulate yourself on your achievements, whatever they were. Give yourself a warm and generous pat on the back.*

Now look back and notice what you haven't accomplished that you had intended to do. Ask yourself: What have I learned from this? Was I over-ambitious with my schedule and do I need to scale down my expectations? Did I get too sidetracked and need to learn to focus? Did I lose track of time? Or worry too much about time?

Now ask yourself: What would enable me to get slightly better at matching my intentions to my actions?

Now, honour all of it as part of your learning, and let it go. No regrets, no blame.

I remember an incredibly busy period years ago, when I went to bed every night feeling bad because I hadn't done everything that needed doing. I suddenly saw that I had to find another way to measure my day than having accomplished everything there was to do. I decided then to set myself reasonable goals and schedules, and to be pleased with myself if I achieved them. It was a total turnaround, and a great joy.

I now also know that if I have my intention clear and my motivation present, unless I am involved in some addictive activity (usually related to the computer), I can trust myself to do what feels right at any time, and know I will end up doing what is needed. In fact, this is how I have managed to write this book, with relatively little stress, but within my self-imposed deadlines.

If you are the sort of person that needs deadlines and no one is setting them from the outside, then find a way to do it for yourself. In order to make sure I finished this book, before I even looked for a publisher, I set a date for my new course on the same subject, and promised the course members that I would have the book finished by that date. I took this as a solid commitment, and I made it happen.

FOCUSING, FOCUSING, FOCUSING
WITH EACH STEP YOU TAKE

Each step you take will work much better if you take a few moments before you do it to visualize it and to get focused and clear.

◆

Try this: When you want to do something, do a quick visualization of yourself doing it perfectly, and seeing how you got there. If you are confused or ambivalent, you could use both futures, yourself feeling good about it, and yourself feeling bad about it, and look back to see the difference in the attitude or steps that took you to the different futures. Often comparing the two really shows you what you need to focus on. Either way, always put the future you want in a bubble, as in Step 7 of this chapter's Spiritual Gym and ask and intend for it to be and release it.

This is also very good when you want to do something – even write a letter or make a phone call – that is weighing on you and goes round and round in your mind.

Try this: *If you need to get out of bed, but don't feel like it, create a pleasant image of yourself up and about and doing something enjoyable, put it in a bubble, intend and release it, as in Step 7 of this chapter's Spiritual Gym, and then wait until you get out of bed naturally. Similarly, if you need to make a phone call in the evening, but are worried about whether you will do it, do the same and then notice that when evening comes you gravitate to the phone to get that call out of the way. Whatever it is that you want to do but find difficult, just allow an image of yourself doing it to emerge on the screen, put the image in the bubble and intend and release it. This reduces anxiety, and gets it out of your mind and into the realm of potential waiting to be actualized. You'll be amazed at how powerfully it works, even when you are feeling hopelessly lazy!*

YOU ARE NOT AN ISLAND

You do need other people. You are not an island.

When you have taken responsibility, done your best and called upon your inner resources, you can surrender and be completely open to help, encouragement and assistance. This is very different from feeling helpless and wanting to be rescued.

One of the striking things in Connie's story is that even though she created a career requiring her to sit at her computer for long hours, and even though she was so very self-directed towards her goal, her life was and is also chock-full of people and more people in every shape, form and relationship.

She knew that to get where she wanted to go, she had to keep connecting to people, books, courses, interviews, mentoring, contacts, clients, colleagues, conferences, and then do it some more to keep expanding and learning. The life she created also had to include people she could be of service to, and time spent with friends and family.

To begin with, Connie didn't even know what her career would be. All she knew was that it had to give her financial security and be able to be conducted from her bedroom if necessary. The rest evolved as she followed the clues until she located what she wanted to do, and then found out how to make it work. She couldn't have done this sitting in front of her computer at home.

You might be more of a loner than this, or need less interaction than this, and that's great too. Or you may know more about where you want to go and how to get there. But creating a new beginning is unlikely to be something you can do completely on your own, nor is your new life likely to be on an island all by yourself.

In order to clarify exactly what you want, to look into how to do it, to explore different avenues, to get support and encouragement, to get practical help and resources, to find out other points of view, or to find colleagues, contacts or clients, you will need to open up to people and keep interacting with them. Whether what you want is a new relationship, a new role, or a new anything else, there is no substitute for setting up as many meetings with relevant people as you can, learning what you can from each person, making all the mistakes and getting all the refusals you can bear, and learning from these too.

So make that phone call, set up that meeting, make that contact. It may be scary the first few times, but eventually you will get how important it is not only for you, but sometimes for the other person too. When I ask people for an interview that I can draw on for my books, for example, it usually turns out that they are delighted to be asked, and that they love seeing the finished description of their journey. It gives them a sense of acknowledgement and pride.

I remember talking to Jack Canfield, the best-selling co-author of the *Chicken Soup for the Soul*[2] series, about how he had got himself to the top of the *New York Times* best-seller list. I later read that he has actually launched 47 *New York Times* best-sellers and sold over 500 million books. One of the things he did before writing *Chicken Soup for the Soul*, he told me, was to contact people who had written *New York Times* best-sellers, and ask for their advice, even if he didn't know them personally. As it turned out, many were happy to be asked, and incredibly helpful to him, and those that refused, refused. He was okay with that.

You may even need to try out a new job or career to see whether it works for you. Many people who start new careers have spent a lot of time trying out different things and finding out what they love before they have settled on one path.

When you have meetings by Skype, or learn by reading a book or by listening to an MP3, it is still to do with people. However, the modern trend towards distance communication won't always serve you, so do also seek out real live people in face-to-face interaction to help you with support, learning or even plain companionship.

I also suggest that you find some consistent support person or people for this difficult thing you are doing, whether it be a mentor, a coach, a peer support group or a buddy. I'll say more about this in the next chapter, but for now, ask yourself, 'Why do it the hard and lonely way if I don't have to?' Maybe that is the way you've always done it, but remember: this is about a new beginning.

BEING PEACEFUL

My friend Geoff once sent me this wonderful Taoist saying that I put up on my wall:

There is so much to do. There is so little time.
We must go slowly.

There is also a story told about Gandhi that he took an hour's walk a day, but when he was too busy to do it, he took two hours.

With these thoughts in mind, remember to build into your life whatever meditation, walking meditation, relaxation, breathing exercise, or Imagework exercise can give you a space in your day that is not about doing. Do it in the morning for 15 minutes. Or do five minutes three times a day. Or do whatever works for you. But do it.

For me, it is crucial to set myself up for the day with a meditation before I do anything else, and for this I do a variation of the meditation I give in the Spiritual Gym Exercise 10 on page 217. Try it.

In the monastery and retreats of the Vietnamese Buddhist Zen Master Thich Nhat Hanh, a bell or a chime or a gong rings about every quarter of an hour. Each time, everyone stops and breathes three times.

When I say everyone, I mean everyone. This includes the office staff, and it includes Thich Nhat Hanh himself when he is giving a talk.

Thay, as Thich Nhat Hanh is called by students and monastics, is prone to say, 'I am happy because I am breathing.'

He is known for doing a slow walking meditation everywhere he goes, anywhere in the world, and stopping regularly to breathe and look within and without. He is never ever seen hurrying. Yet he has accomplished a remarkable amount in his life, written wonderful books, inspired people all over the world, and set up core practices that have changed the lives of many. In fact, he was one of the first to bring the concept of mindfulness to the West.

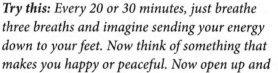

Try this: Every 20 or 30 minutes, just breathe three breaths and imagine sending your energy down to your feet. Now think of something that makes you happy or peaceful. Now open up and listen within, or look around at the beauty around you. There is actually an app on the I-phone

called 'Mindfulness Bell' that you can set to ring as often as you wish. I love it. I set it to ring every 20 minutes, and it reminds me to stop and breathe and come back to myself.

***Try this**: To do a walking meditation, take one step, breathing in, next step, breathing out, and just keep going like that, one step one breath. Do this for 15 minutes a day if you can and you will find your whole system slowing down and becoming peaceful. If possible, walk somewhere you find beautiful, but do it even if you are stuck in your office.*

You could try saying this little refrain by Thay to yourself as you walk:

(Breathing in, taking a step) Peace is the breath.

(Breathing out, taking a step) Happiness is the walking.

And this can work for you whenever you are walking anywhere. If you need to actually go somewhere, you can make it three or four steps per outbreath, or even more. (It is better to extend your outbreath than your inbreath.) As long as you keep being aware of the breath, and staying in rhythm with it, no matter how fast you need to go, you are never in a hurry.

In fact, get in the habit of doing a walking meditation when you walk from room to room at home or at work. You'll be amazed at how different you will feel.

The busier you are, the more you have to do this. It is your protection, and your joy.

Thay talks of the time that he received word that he and his whole community would have to leave the country they were living in by the following day.

He said to himself, 'If there is no peace now, there is no peace.' And with this in mind, he did a walking meditation all night, and by morning he knew what to do.

If there is no peace now, there is no peace... I remind myself of this whenever I move into a mad hurry and panic. It instantly quietens me down. I slow down and breathe deeply.

THE JOY BEYOND ALL UNDERSTANDING

I like to think about cultivating what I call the *joy beyond all understanding*, i.e. the joy that fills you at a deep level no matter what is going on in the world or in your world.

Every now and then ask yourself, 'Where is my joy?' and find it. Do make sure to surround yourself with things that give you joy, and consciously give yourself at least three joyful moments a day. Do this even if you are depressed and don't believe you have any joy. Just tell yourself that three joy moments is enough. To be fully in touch with your joy, you need to step back for a moment, and have some space in your mind and heart. Joy flourishes in spaciousness.

Then at night, when you are lying in bed, try reflecting for a moment on these questions:

◆ What is one thing I did towards my vision?
◆ What is one thing I did for others?
◆ What were my three moments of joy?

Whatever the answers, smile lovingly at yourself each time and say, 'Well done' and 'I love you.'

Then consider what you are looking forward to tomorrow, including simply meeting life in all its wonder. And smile again.

The power of the smile is great indeed.

Your Spiritual Gym
Exercise 9:
Getting Practical

Materials needed: Paper and pen, or a computer if that is easier for you. You might also want to print out weekly, monthly and yearly calendars to help you see the lay of the land visually.

If you can, do this exercise with a friend or colleague, particularly someone who is a bit knowledgeable either about your area or about project management to help you tease out the details of your plan.

1. Do you have a time frame for getting to your vision? What period of time did you go forward to in your visioning? This is a good clue. Imagine a line on the floor that starts with the beginning date (preferably today or tomorrow or right after your holiday) and ends at the date you set as the achievement of the vision. Make sure it is realistic. Try doubling the time period and see if that is more realistic. We will call this your time line.

2. Now, step on at the beginning of the time line and take three or four steps, or however many you feel you need. Each step, you step forward one foot, bring your feet together, breathe, listen within and sense what that step is. If possible, say it aloud as it comes to you. Sometimes the speaking itself gives you the answer. What is your first step, your second, your third, and more if there are more? Where are they on the time line? If you are

working with a buddy, have them write it down for you. Otherwise, sit down afterwards and write them down, including the timing, As one student wrote to me, 'I found the timeline had a kind of "magic" about it, and that it knew things about my future that I didn't.'

3. Now plan the sub-steps you need to accomplish those major steps. Whom do I need to meet? What research do I need to do? When do I need to make final decisions? Clarify how much time each one of these will take. I sometimes find it helpful to make a list of all of these sub-tasks on the one side, and the number of hours or days I have in reality to accomplish them (e.g. you may have two months, but in that time, how many hours per day, and how many days per month are actually available). Then I just look at the two lists, and either cross out items on one side, or add time at the end of the other. I always assume I have given myself too much to do!

4. Create an approximate timetable for the activities, knowing that it will change. It can be a weekly, monthly and/or yearly one depending on the tasks and your temperament. Know that more things will emerge as you go along, and that you may well need to relax your deadlines. Now walk through the time line again, saying, if possible aloud, what you are doing at each point. Let yourself feel great as you do it.

5. Now stand at the end point and celebrate your new life. Say where you are, how good you feel and what you have

accomplished. Don't plan what you will say, but see what emerges. It will be something like: It is 20XX and this is my new life. I feel great and this is what is happening. (e.g. 'It is 2015 and this is my new life: I have had my first art exhibition, and feel really proud of how many paintings I have sold.' Or 'It is 2014 and this is my new life: I am living with my new partner and about to go on a trip together and I feel delighted with how life has turned out.' Or whatever your new beginning is).

6. Now do the bubble exercise again:

   a. See yourself having accomplished everything you have set out to accomplish, looking happy, proud, contented, or whatever emotion seems to come, and put this picture in a bubble.

   b. Ask yourself if you are willing to follow through consistently and do your best, and also to be open to any help from others or from the universe. In other words: are you willing to show willing? If so, say, aloud if possible, 'I ask and intend for this to be.'

   c. Ask yourself if you are also willing to acknowledge that this is not all up to you, and that you are willing to surrender to that which goes beyond you, including your unconscious, fate, luck, the universe, God, or whatever you believe in. If so, say, aloud if possible, 'I release it.'

    d. Blow the bubble out with a strong expulsive breath into the domain of potential waiting to be actualized. If you are working with a buddy, you can put both bubbles into a larger bubble, and blow it out together.

    e. Stand up, and say, aloud if at all possible, with all the power you can muster, 'So must it be NOW' and during the NOW make a strong gesture with your arm and stamp your foot. This needs to have so much power that it feels as if you are commanding the universe within and without to obey. You may need to try three or four times until you feel something really transform inside you, as if the molecules are reordering themselves!

7. Do this bubble exercise each time you start a new activity or phase, particularly if you have any doubts or confusion about it. This will help you align yourself with confidence so that you will be working with a very high level of focus to reach your goals.

8. It also helps, as you accomplish bits of your plan, to congratulate yourself, and put a tick or some symbol by the original listing so that you can see yourself eating up the miles towards your goal. Better yet, put up a chart on your fridge and give yourself gold stars! If you find you are not accomplishing everything you hope or in the time frame you hope, you need to look at it again, and rethink and replan. Have you simply put too much in? Or is there something you need to do to tighten your

focus? This schedule is not a prison, but a constantly changing and evolving plan that responds to who you are, and what is coming towards you in the world.

9. You may find, as I have, that when your intentions are absolutely clear and unambivalent, and you are not being addictive about anything, that you will naturally and intuitively do what is right for you at any time, even if it is not how you foresaw it, and that will work. If you are ambivalent, or get addictively involved whether in computer games, emails, drink, drugs, TV or whatever is your thing, then your intuition will not be so clear in your everyday life. So get clear, and life gets much easier!

CHAPTER 10

Divining, Deciding, Delivering, Doing and Delighting

When I was about six years old, I believed that one day Tony, the school bus driver, would come to my house and ring my bell and say, 'Because you've been such a good girl, I've got a present for you, a magic box.' The box would have a magic wand inside, and when I waved it, everything I wished for would come true.

Now I think of it, even when I was making a wish on my birthday cakes, I never 'wasted' my wish on anything specific. I thought I might as well wish that everything I wished for would come true. I was quite rational in a magical kind of way.

I used to work out variations in my mind to make the wand even more perfect, such as that it would only grant my wish if it was good for me, or that I could make smaller wands for my friends.

Then one day I sat up in bed and said to myself, 'But that's magic and I don't believe in magic.'

And that was that.

And yet, it is quite clear that working with the imagination as I do, I am still rational in a magical sort of way. In fact, I specialize in teaching people how to create inner magic wands that will not only get them what they want, but even help them see if it is right for them.

That is what this book, and indeed all my books and courses, are about.

You have now begun to create the magic box of your imagination. You can carry this within you for the rest of your life, and tap into it at will to protect and guide yourself towards that which your heart and soul desire, as well as to inspire you to do what you need to do to get there.

It's all there, asking to be called upon.

You are the one you have been waiting for.

SANDWICHES FOR THE TRIP

This chapter has even more '*Try this*' exercises scattered through it than ever.

This is my way of trying to give you sandwiches for the trip.

If this is mixing metaphors too much, you can think of it as a few different spells to use when you wave your magic wand.

Either way, take this chapter *really* slowly, and stop to try out all these different things. Some of them will work for you and some won't. Decide to incorporate the ones that work well for you into your life and to use them on a regular basis.

THE HOLISTIC WAY OF LIFE

Perhaps the next challenge is to create a life that is made up of more of the elements that you need so that you can feel happy and fulfilled. If you've been one-sided, can you become many-sided? If you've been too much of a butterfly, can you begin to focus on your priorities in a consistent way?

In other words, whatever has been undeveloped or underdeveloped in your old life needs to be given room to breathe and grow.

It is interesting to look back at Connie's story (see page 171) and compare her old life and her new life:

Connie's old life: I thought there must be some other way to live than to be gone from your house 12–14 hours a day 6–7 days a week. I left at the crack of dawn and then after school I went to real estate appointments. I couldn't physically continue at the pace I was going just to pay the bills. I had missed every event with my family and friends.

Connie's new life: A typical day is this – I work from 6.30–10 am, including weekends, on work to do with my business. I'm gone from the house by 10 am, doing things in the community, different projects to do with charities. I holiday about four times a year with family and friends. I'm also travelling every month and combining work events with pleasure.

In other words, Connie not only created a way of working that fitted her needs, but she made sure that she didn't get lost in the new work. She used the leverage of the money she was earning to make her life work for her as a whole, so that she could do what she loved as well as what supported her financially.

STELLA'S STORY

My client Stella, a beautiful and successful arts and culture consultant, does not strike anyone who meets her as the slightest bit physically disabled. Yet at age 17 she was diagnosed with severe rheumatoid arthritis, and told that if she didn't take the drugs prescribed to her, she'd be in a wheelchair all her life. Of course, if she did take them, she'd be very ill from the side-effects of the drugs. Stella carries her illness so lightly, that it was not until I 'googled' it and saw the photos of people with advanced rheumatoid arthritis that I realized how very disabling the natural course of her illness is expected to be, and how miraculous is her level of health and wellbeing.

This is her story of how she found her way to a holistic and balanced way of living. It is a classic story of the journey from difficult times through a turning point to a new beginning:

I was 17 and diagnosed with severe rheumatoid arthritis. This was after months in which my body packed up, and I went from being extremely physically active to not being able to be active at all. Everything ached and I couldn't move easily. Nobody knew what was wrong with me and it was really tough.

Then I was diagnosed and there was a period of about a year when I became a patient, someone who had to go to the doctor once a week for an injection. I was told that I had to take meds with severe side-effects, and with that knowledge came a healthy bout of depression.

I'd lost pretty much everything. I had been a dancer, doing ballet two or three times a week since the age of six, and it was my life outside of school and I was very good at it. I'd stopped but now I couldn't dance even if I wanted to and this was demoralizing. After the first year that I was medicated, depressed and with a real sense of loss, I decided I wanted to change that way of being and I was going to look for other answers.

I wasn't willing to accept this as the only way without finding out for myself.

That led me to a path of beginning to meet other practitioners. I went to see a homeopath and after a month of seeing him, he wanted me to stop all the meds. I went to see the consultant rheumatologist at the hospital, and said I would like to stop the treatment.

His answer was that if I stopped I'd be in a wheelchair in six months.

I walked out of the hospital in tears and called the homeopath and asked him to find me a consultant who was open to another way. That phone call was a pivotal moment I have never forgotten. At the age of 18, telling a professor of medicine that you're not happy takes a level of courage.

The homeopath then referred me to a consultant in Croydon who'd done the research on the connection between food and arthritis and was more than happy for me to go on a diet rather than take medication.

I started the journey of finding out more about my body, going to the allergy clinic, and actually accepting that I was different and had to learn what it was my body needed and what it didn't want.

It was and still is a long journey. But I'm not taking a whole load of toxic medication and I didn't end up in a wheelchair.

Mentally there's something about knowing you can be in control of the reactions of your body rather than existing in the unknown as in conventional treatment. There's no cure and all conventional medicine can do is suppress the immune system so it doesn't react, and this has other effects. I was never well, and actually never knew if I was going to wake up unable to walk.

I've built a team of amazing therapists who help me look after myself, ranging from the immunologist to the T'ai Chi master, acupuncturist, masseuse and psychotherapist. And I'm actually very fit. I've had a knee replacement and lots of surgery, but my spirit isn't broken, and it's not a continuous degeneration, which is the sentence they give you in conventional medicine. In fact, nobody who meets me would know there was anything wrong with me unless they saw the scars.

This has shown me that there are always other options and I need to have the courage to say so. It also reinforced a level of courage at not being willing to accept a negative prognosis. And standing up for myself.

It's also made me aware at a very early age of how important it is to look after my body but also to nurture my soul as much as my body, because they go hand in hand. My T'ai Chi practice, and the recognition of nurturing the soul are probably two of the most important things in making the shift. I'm forced to accept that I'm not purely a machine and there has to be a level of balance in my life.

Now more than ever, there's the T'ai Chi or meditation in the morning, and making sure that I've got the right food so that I'm not going to run on empty, and constantly listening to my body, mind and soul. There's a level of acceptance of my needs after being rebellious about it. I know it's the right thing to do and that's very different from being told what to do.

And I've learned that there's not only one way of being. That's what holistic is to me. It's not just about the rule and the law. It's about what you need, and what suits me might not suit someone else. We're all individuals and you need to find the right way of being for you.

Stella's story is remarkable, but more remarkable even than she herself has realized. Like so many people suffering pain, loss and disability, it was so important to her to be treated normally and with respect, that she never allowed herself to think about how tough it all was. It is not until now that she has been able to admit to herself how big a challenge she has faced, how painful it has been, and how much energy it has taken up in her life. She is beginning to acknowledge what a hard road she travels, how much she needs to care for herself and honour herself on her journey, and how willing she needs to be vulnerable and even to ask for help, something she's never really done. She is finally learning, on a profound level, how to combine compassion for her limitation and pain, and respect for her magnificence.

She considers this to be her *new* new beginning.

ALL OUR DIMENSIONS

We live in a time when we are called upon to develop all our dimensions at once – personal and social, male and female, inner and outer, physical and emotional, social and spiritual – and yet we each need to find our own way to do that. We don't know how to do it, we can't follow any one set of rules, and we may be painfully full of blockages on various levels.

Don't turn these aspirations into monsters that haunt you or taunt you with not being good enough. None of us knows how to do it, and we are all on a steep learning curve.

But do keep an eye on the challenge of living a holistic life that expresses more of you than perhaps you have heretofore done, as well as keeping you healthy and nourished on every level. This was what Stella was forced to learn at a young age, pushed by serious physical illness. But eventually, we do all need to learn it, and why not sooner rather than later?

In fact, why not right now?

JOY, CHALLENGE AND WELLBEING

Think of it this way:

- Your joy is a guide to bringing more of what you love into your life.
- Your sense of challenge and accomplishment is a guide to what could expand you.
- Your sense of wellbeing is a guide to what nourishes you.

Try this: You can check out your life from this point of view, like measuring your temperature, by just asking yourself about different activities:

How much joy do I have from this? (1–10),

How much challenge? (1–10)

How much nourishment and wellbeing? (1–10).

The range of 6–8 is quite a good one to go for – neither a low nor a high, but just full of goodness.

Whatever number comes up, ask yourself these two questions, and just wait for an answer to come from within: What would it take to raise this number just half a point? And what would it take to raise it to 10?

Take seriously the answers that come, and consider following through.

You can also look more generally at the pattern of your life. Where is your joy in your life right now? And where is your growing edge? And how do your roots get nourished?

◆

Try this: Draw a picture of a tree that somehow represents you in your new life. Now name the branches, the trunk and the roots. Show what the fruits are and where your nourishment is.

To expand your thinking about what would fill your life with joy, try thinking past your present life constraints to remember what is really important to you.

Try this: Write at the top of a page 'Ten Things I Want to Do Before I Die' and then start listing whatever comes to mind. If you have an Imagework buddy, you can read each other the question and write it down for each other. Then choose one of these that you can do in whole or in part in the next six months. Can you commit yourself to doing it? If so, say aloud, 'I will xxxxx.'

Your soul community

You need people who help you do what you want to do, as we talked of in the last chapter, but you also need people who simply honour you and love you for who you are and who you are becoming, rather than for your roles and achievements.

This means that in among all the meetings we talked of in the last chapter that are goal related, you also need to create for yourself, if you don't already have it, a group of people that recognize who and what you are and are becoming, and whom you similarly recognize. They are members of what I call your 'soul community'.

If you have people who are important to you, yet you've never told them about the things that you really care about, then try it. Some will get it, and will become part of your soul community. Others won't, but they are still your friends or family, and precious in that way.

One lovely thing to set up is Co-listening, a method of focused talking and listening that is truly transformative. You can have a single Co-listening partner or a Co-listening group, which we call in Skyros an *oekos* group or home group. I've always had one or the other or both in my life.

I will introduce it briefly here, but do go to my website http://www.dinaglouberman.com/approach/co-listening/ to find out more about it. Read the summary and at the bottom of the page, you will find a link to download a free pdf with the instructions for Co-listening.

Try this: The principle of Co-listening is simple, though it is easy to get tripped up. It is a method of what I call Real Talk and Real Listening. In other words, when you are being speaker, you open up and speak from your heart, and when you are being the listener, you open up and listen from your heart to what the other person is saying, both with total focus and without judgement. Everything has

to be kept in strict time, because you each need to have equal time.

Have a meeting face-to-face, if at all possible, or by phone or Skype if necessary, with one or more people that you want to share with on a deep level. Agree on the time you have, divide it equally with some time left over at the end.

Each person has 5–15 minutes, depending on your time constraints, to take three slow breaths and say whatever comes to their mind and heart on the deepest level they can get to, without planning or censoring. The listeners also take three breaths, and then just open up and listen.

After each talk period, there is feedback, probably no more than five minutes, which has simple rules for the listener who is giving the feedback to keep it all very safe:

♦ You sum up what you thought the speaker said, not covering everything, but just the main point or points you were left with. 'What I'm left with is…' Check if the speaker agrees. If not, you accept what they say, and don't insist you know better even if you think you do.

♦ You can also say what you felt, (e.g. I felt connected to you, sad, angry on your behalf etc). Remember that if you say, 'I felt that…', it is a thought or judgement and not a feeling, so don't go there!

What is not allowed? No criticism, no rescuing, no interpreting and no advice. Do check the website details to see what this means exactly. You are simply being present with the other or others and hearing what they are saying. You are not 'helping' them.

Then the other or others do the same. At the end you have time for everyone to share a bit about what you are left with about yourself and the other people.

The power of this is that you have an opportunity to share and listen on such a deep level that as speaker you find a way through any difficulties or confusions naturally; as listener you are able to be really present on a profound heart and soul level, and there is a deepening connection and trust between all those involved.

Try this: *If you are working with this person or group as a part of moving forward in your life, do a new round where you each decide on an intention that you will carry out before the next meeting. Then when the next meeting comes, you use this second round to say how you did with your intention, and if you didn't carry it out, think about the reason for that as honestly as you can, whether it is to do with the over-ambitiousness of the plan or your own motivation to procastinate.*

Then set a new intention, or perhaps a more realistic version of the first one, to carry out before you meet again.

Please don't be so afraid to tell your group you haven't done it that you miss the meeting! If you can let yourself be honest and courageous, seeing yourself with compassion and respect, this method will take you a long way.

You may have noticed that I dedicated this book to my soul community. This doesn't consist only of people who are alive and in my life. It includes all the people, books, images and wise beings I talk to or learn from or teach, whether on an inner or an outer level, whether they are in this dimension or another. In other words, it includes all those who in some way share or support the path of learning, love and truth that I am on.

Because of my soul community, I am never alone. And I do not fear death because I believe I will be accompanied by members of my soul community on this side and the other.

It's quite a community. I feel very honoured to have it.

And so will you.

DIVINING, DECIDING, DOING, DELIVERING, DELIGHTING

We are approaching the time that this trajectory from difficult times to new beginnings comes to resolution, delivers the goods, leaves you feeling proud of your achievements and about to consider what's next.

If you look back at the path you have been on, you can see the steps of what is essentially a creative process, which can be summed up as: divining, deciding, doing, delivering and delighting.

Divining was your turning point, and that was when you accepted where you were, sank into another level of you, and summoned a vision to show you where you might go.

In order to divine what it is we are being called on to do, we need first to call on the divine in us, that which precedes the conscious plans and judgements we have about what we should be doing. To put it another way, we need to use our divining rod to locate where the water of life is under the surface.

From divination you moved to deciding. That was when you chose your path, said *Yes*, and committed to put your wholehearted energy into it and go for it. Energy follows thought, but you need to choose to support this natural process with your conscious will.

Then and only then came the doing. The doing was part of a plan, made sense, fitted into a larger purpose, and was helped along by that which is beyond you. It was not just an endless list of 'To Dos' that never gets any shorter! And it promised a good chance of success, though no guarantees.

After the doing comes the delivering. Hopefully, you are either at that stage, or can see the possibility of it. You tie the package up and deliver it, or it is delivered to you. Here it is, the completed act, the new beginning, that which you pictured and brought into being. There is a moment of grace when you complete something that needs to be honoured.

In that honouring of what you have delivered or had delivered to you comes the delight. This stage is crucial and one we often forget. You need to celebrate that creation, and appreciate yourself and all those who helped along the way. Please also give yourself time to enjoy, integrate and rest before the next process starts. Without this, you are back on that old treadmill. There is no joy, and therefore no real reason to continue.

It is especially important to stay conscious of this if you are inclined to think that emptiness and space are an affront and need to be filled immediately!

If you are not yet at this stage, picture it, and then come back to this chapter again later. If what you have tried to do has not succeeded, then it is time to accept where you are, and vision the next creative journey that might work better. It is after all the journey that you were committed to, not the fruits of your labour, which you could never predict and control with certainty.

WHERE ARE YOU NOW?

With all the inner and outer changes you have been going through, it is good to check in on a deep level where you are in yourself at this moment and how it compares to where you've been.

It could be time for another Image as Life Metaphor exercise (see page 64) and another visioning (see page 139) to find out where you are now, what your next step is, and what it is that you want for your life in the days and months to come. Remember that you need an inner map not just to get out of a hole, but to navigate the way ahead with joy and confidence. Consider doing this regularly, or every time you feel your current vision has come to resolution one way or another, and you need a new inspiration. I do the Image as Life Metaphor exercise any time I am puzzled as to what is happening, and the visioning as often as I need it to set my course. And whenever I facilitate an imagery group, I always take the opportunity to do all the exercises myself.

Once you are stabilizing into a new life, it becomes particularly important not to just coast and get into old patterns. So it is good to check in with yourself daily and weekly as well as to set your visioning for longer periods.

Getting on track is vital. Staying on track, or rather coming back when you stray, is miraculous.

To tune into yourself daily, and also to look at the day ahead, I strongly suggest the morning meditation/ visualization you will find in the Spiritual Gym for this chapter. I do a version of this every day, and it keeps me clear, focused and set for a good day. It also develops a new structure of consciousness, where you become aware of aligning your mind, emotion and body with the whispers of your heart and soul, you choose each day to have a good day that ends well, and you know you can always go back to the peace and joy beyond all understanding whatever is happening in your everyday life.

I always say to my students: Do this every day for a month, and it will change your life, or rather, your way of experiencing your life. Then if it works for you at least half as well as I say it will, keep going.

I've seen the powerful effect as people shift their focus and live from the inside out with joy as well as a profound confidence that they are on the right track and at their best.

FIVE THINGS FOR JOY

Here's also something I love to do weekly to keep me on track and taking care of the important things. Why not try it?

◆

Try this: At the beginning of each week, sit down and take three pages, and put one heading on each page:

- ◆ Five things I will do for joy.
- ◆ Five things I will do towards my goals.
- ◆ Five things I will do for others.

Now, make a list of five things under each category. Try not to think too hard, just write what comes to mind.

At the end of the week, tick the ones you did or partially did. And even if you did only one of them, congratulate yourself. Look at the pattern of what you did most of and what you did least of. Consider what this tells you, and what you want for next week.

Enjoy all of it, not just the joyful bits. They are all part of being you.

TAKE YOURSELF SERIOUSLY, TAKE YOURSELF LIGHTLY

This is just a reminder that you matter, and that you make a difference. Therefore you need to take yourself seriously enough to do what is necessary to become the person you want to become. What you do and are and become will have a ripple effect all around you, so make that ripple effect a positive one.

Susan, a young client of mine, has worked with me for over two years, and consistently taken the work seriously and done her 'homework'. In that time she has grown from a child to an adult woman, from being in a rather lost and depressed state to feeling in charge of her life and training for a career she loves.

What she is now finding is that as she stops being the designated problem child, her whole family is transforming before her eyes, though she is seemingly the only one who has been doing the personal and spiritual development.

Her parents are more aware and open than they've ever been and are willing to be more honest about what has gone on in the family. Her sister, on the other hand, who used to be considered the healthy, happy one, is now showing the cracks in her armour, clearly signalling that she needs help and that she will eventually go for it. The relatives and friends of the family whose shoulders she used to cry on sometimes phone to get advice from her.

Susan is seeing that she is now an adult and has a positive influence on people she loves, and that this is her new stage in life. It's a rather wonderful moment.

I hasten to say that this is not about you being a *Very Important Person* who takes themselves *Very Seriously Indeed.*

Can you take yourself seriously on a soul level and take yourself lightly as an ordinary punter doing your best in a difficult world? It's a bit like seeing yourself with compassion and respect. You are magnificent, and you also have loads of pain and limitations.

Is that okay with you? I hope so. Being human is always a challenge to our fragile egos.

THE STORY EMERGES IN THE TELLING

At this moment of embarking on your new beginning, it is helpful to remember that there is more to life than you know right now, or indeed will ever know. The story will emerge in the telling and you can never know how it will turn out.

Getting where you want to go is useful, but at the same time it limits you to the boundaries of your present imagination.

Yes, you had to sense what was right on the deepest possible level, using all the power of your rational and intuitive minds, and go for it. You have done this. But even if you have achieved everything you set out to achieve, you still need to leave room also for the miracle, the process that you couldn't have predicted. Whatever it is, and whether it seems wonderful or terrible, it will always be interesting and always challenge you to take your next step.

My friend Lois passed on this little mantra: *I expect a miracle.* I love it. Try saying it a few times and see what happens.

I find that whether or not I literally have more miracles, I notice so many more of the miracles of life itself.

With an attitude of true surrender to the miracle of life, you can celebrate your fumbling states and your place of not knowing, the failures and the successes, the wonder of the struggle and the power of your creativity.

Even when the anxiety or the shoulds or the self-doubts or the rage or the humiliation overwhelm you, you can remind yourself that you haven't got it wrong but are simply facing the challenge of being human.

This is how it is to be human. This is how it is to be open to life. And knowing this, you will be able to use your creativity to get you through.

ALL OF YOU

Whether your boat is sailing somewhere new, or resting in the harbour, it is still and always your life. Taking responsibility for that life is about embracing all of you, from the soul's whispers to the child's tantrums to your heart's joy.

Is this practical or even possible?

Yes and No.

No, because you are being called to the impossible task of living on all levels at once.

Yes, because you never have to do it perfectly.

And yes again, because you can do it one step at a time.

Your Spiritual Gym
Exercise 10:
Morning Meditation and Visualization

This meditation, plus the brief imagery exercise at the end, is a wonderful beginning to the day. If you feel you don't have time for the whole meditation, you can do any of the parts by themselves. But do the whole thing a few times so that you know what works best for you. And remember, that you don't have to believe in the soul or in sending love and you can just see it all as an image. You only need to be willing to suspend judgement and go with it. As always, you can download an MP3 from my website (http://www.dinaglouberman.com/shop/#cd-list) to be guided through it.

Begin with a brief relaxation, perhaps something like this: Allow your eyes to close and begin to notice your breathing. Allow your breathing to become deeper and slower. Imagine your eyelids are so heavy you couldn't lift them even if you tried. Now allow the heaviness to flow down through your body into the ground, and a lightness come up from the ground through your body, and then out, as if through a hole in the top of your head.

PART ONE: CALL AND RESPONSE BETWEEN THE SOUL AND THE EVERYDAY PERSONALITY (MIND/EMOTION/BODY)
(*OM is a kind of mystic Sanskrit sound, with the quality of universal essence, and powerful to say out loud.*)

1. I imagine a large light behind me, larger than life itself. I will call this the soul. This light is breathing. I don't have to breathe; the light is breathing me. I become the breathing light itself. I say *Om* as if from the soul, calling on the mind, emotion and body to come home. *Om*.

2. I focus on the mind. 'My mind says…'(finish the sentence spontaneously). I wash the mind with light, cleaning and clearing until I am left only with the *truth that has no words*. I stay with that truth for a moment. I say *Om* from the larger mind, responding to the call of the soul that I am coming home. *Om*.

3. I focus on the emotions. 'My emotions say…' I wash the emotions with light, until I am left only with the *peace and joy beyond all understanding*. I stay with that peace and joy for a moment. I say *Om* from the emotions, responding to the soul that I am coming home. *Om*.

4. I focus on my physical body and I also imagine an energy body or light body around it. 'My body says…' I wash my body with light, clearing any blocked pathways in the energy body and stimulating and revitalizing the physical body. I say *Om* from the body, responding to the soul that I am coming home. *Om*.

5. I come back to the soul, becoming the light with mind, emotions and body all together all aligned and working as a team. The soul says… I say *Om* as if from the soul, with mind, emotion and body all resonating together. *Om*.

Part Two: The master in the heart

I focus on my heart and imagine a closed golden lotus flower. As I breathe into it, it reveals an electric blue centre. Once the flower is open, I allow to emerge an image of a master or teacher or guide or of my own soul. (This could be anyone from Archangel Michael to your grandmother.) I discover their qualities, and dwell in their presence. I might ask a question, or just wait for a message, which can be verbal or non-verbal. I then find their qualities in me, seeing the master or guide as my true mirror. Then I thank them and say goodbye.

Part Three: Gratitude and guiding light

I welcome the day, and say 'Thank You for the day,' not because of the content, but just for the fact that I have a new fresh day, 24 hours to breathe and to love life. I send the light and life of the soul as a beam of light over my path for the day to protect and guide me. I stand under that light for a moment and see what my focus needs to be.

May the energy of the soul fill me, and may I express that radiance in joyous living.

(Later on in the day if you get confused or unfocused, imagine standing under this light to get focus and guidance.)

Part Four: Visioning the day

It's the end of the day and I feel good. What's the good feeling? What's the main thing I feel good about? As I look back on the day, what did I do to get myself here? Now I come back to the present. I put the future in a bubble in my hand. I ask and intend for this to be. And I release it.

Now I blow the bubble out into the domain of potential waiting to be actualized, and I take the future feeling into my heart and feel it now.

Thank you. It is already so. (Or: *So must it be. NOW*)

Part Five: Sending love

I say *Om* three times, and with the first *Om* send love and light to my loved ones, with the second *Om*, to all the people who are on this path of learning with me, including teachers and colleagues and students, and with the third *Om* to all of humanity, and to the earth and all its creatures. *Om. Om. Om.*

I sit for a moment in the light that has been created, imagining myself in a tent of light from above, and a tent of light from below, from the earth. This can be a good time to shed light on any issues that are concerning you.

Finally: counting up

I'm going to count up from 1–5 and when I say '5', I'm going to open my eyes, relaxed and alert, bringing the peace and wisdom back with me. 1-2-eyelids lightening, 3-4 coming to the surface. 5. Eyes open. I stamp my feet and come back to the room. Three stamps.

REFERENCES

INTRODUCTION

1. Glouberman, Dina, *Life Choices, Life Changes: Develop your Personal Vision with Imagework,*, London: Skyros Books (2010)

CHAPTER 1: SEEING YOUR WAY TO NEW BEGINNINGS

1. Glouberman, Dina, 'Turning Points,' *I-to-I* magazine, 1992–1995

2. Glouberman, Dina, 'The Rebellious Vicar: Turning Points Interview with Chad Varah,' *I-to-I* magazine, Jan–March, 1994, pp.20-21

3. Skyros Holistic Holidays, founded in 1979 by Dr Dina Glouberman and Dr Yannis Andricopoulos, now in Greece, Thailand, Cambodia and Cuba, www.skyros.com

4. Glouberman, Dina, *The Joy of Burnout: How the End of the World can be a New Beginning*, London: Skyros Books (2007)

CHAPTER 2: HOW YOUR WORST ENEMY CAN BE YOUR BEST FRIEND

1. Lakoff, G. & Johnson, M., *Metaphors We Live By.* Chicago: University of Chicago Press (1980)

2. Freud S. (1953). 'The interpretation of dreams' in J. Strachey (Ed & Trans.) *The Standard Edition of the Complete Psychological Works of Sigmund Freud.* (Vol. 4-5, pp. 1-627). London: Hogarth; Jung C.G. (1954) *The Archetypes and the Collective Unconscious. The Collected Works of C.G. Jung,* Vol. 9. New Jersey: Princeton University Press; Perls, F., *Gestalt Therapy Verbatim.* Moab, Utah, Real People Press (1969)

3. Stigler, M. & Pokorny, D. (2001). 'Emotions and primary process in guided imagery psychotherapy: Computerised text-analytic measures', *Psychotherapy Research*, 11(4), pp. 415-431.Decety, J, Jeannerod, M, Durozard, D, Bayerel, G. 'Central Activation of autonomic effectors during mental simulation of motor actions in man'. *Journal of Physiology* (1993) 461, pp.549-563 ; Deschaumes-Molinaro C, Dittmar A, Vernet-Maury E. Autonomic nervous system response patterns correlate with mental imagery. Physiol. Behav. 1992 May;51 (5):1021-7; Deschaumes-Molinaro C, Dittmar A, Vernet-Maury E. 'Relationship between Mental Imagery and Sporting Performance', Behav. Brain Res. 1991Oct. 25;45(1) 29-36; 'A Study of Mental Imagery in Psychotherapy: Constructing a Theoretical Model'; Thomas, V. (2011). 'The therapeutic functions of mental imagery in

psychotherapy: Constructing a theoretical model'. Unpublished D Psych thesis. Held in Middlesex University e-repository at: http://eprints.mdx.ac.uk/10561

4. Gallese, V. & Lakoff, G.,'The brain's concepts: The role of the sensory-motor system in conceptual knowledge,' *Journal of Cognitive Neuropsychology* 22(3/4), pp. 455-479 (2005)

5. Vinoth K. Ranganathan, Vlodek Siemionowa,, Jing Z. Liua, Vinod Sahgal, Guang H. Yuea, 'From mental power to muscle power – gaining strength by using the mind', *Neuropsychoplogia*, 43, 2004, pp. 944-955; Thomas, V. (2011)

6. Glouberman, Dina, *Life Choices, Life Changes: Develop your Personal Vision with Imagework,* London: Skyros Books (2010)

7. Glouberman, Dina, *Life Choices, Life Changes: Develop your Personal Vision with Imagework,* London: Skyros Books (2010)

8. Atsitsa is a branch of Skyros Holistic Holidays, www.skyros.com

9. http://www.dinaglouberman.com/courses-coaching/courses/

10. Hackmann, A., Bennet-Levy, J, Holmes, E.A., *Oxford Guide to Imagery in Cognitive Therapy*, Oxford: Oxford University Press (2011)

11.'What Life Means to Einstein: An Interview by George Sylvester Viereck', *The Saturday Evening Post,* p.17 (26 October 1929)

CHAPTER 3: DIFFICULT TIMES MAKE CHANGE EASY

1. Glouberman, Dina, *The Joy of Burnout: How the End of the World can be a New Beginning,* London: Skyros Books (2007)

2. Caplan, G., *Principles of Preventive Psychiatry*. New York: Basic Books (1964)

CHAPTER 4: STOP, GIVE UP HOPE AND KEEP THE FAITH

1. Hoeg, P., *Miss Smilla's Feeling for Snow*, Vintage, p.39 (2005)

CHAPTER 5: I'M STILL THERE

1. Crisp, Tony, *Dream Dictionary*, Bantam Doubleday Dell Publishing Group (1998)

2. Ram Dass, *Still Here: Embracing Aging, Changing and Dying*, Riverhead Books (2001)

3. Frankl, Victor, *Man's Search for Meaning*, London: Rider (2004)

4. Wilhelm, R. Translation, The I Ching or Book of Changes, NY: Bollingen Foundation, p.16 (1950)

Chapter 6: Expand, Don't Contract

1. Glouberman, Dina, "Leaping off the Edge: Turning Points Interview with Gabrielle Roth', *I-to-I* magazine, Jan.-March, 1995, pp.21-23
2. Glouberman, Dina, 'Adding Layers to the Onion: Turning Points Interview with Michael York', *I-to-I* magazine, Jan.-March 1992, pp.16-17

Chapter 7: Visioning for Dummies

1. Skyros Holistic Holidays, www.skyros.com

Chapter 8: Saying Yes

1. Bly, Robert, *Iron John*, London: Rider (2004)
2. Glouberman, Dina, 'Who will protect you when the burglar breaks in: Turning Points Interview with Robert Bly', *I-to-I* magazine, Oct–Dec, 1991, pp.18-19
3. Gawain, Shakti, *Creative Visualization*, New World Library (2002) (first published 1978)
4. Glouberman, Dina, 'I'm not enlightened: Turning Points Interview with Shakti Gawain', *I-to-I* magazine, July–Sept, 1994, pp.28-29
5. Glouberman, Dina, 'I would love myself unconditionally if only I were different…' *I-to-I* magazine, November, 1990, pp.16-17
6. See www.aaron.com for his general approach
7. To go into more detail about the process of moving from what you want to what you choose, and the power of this, do see Robert Fritz (1986) *The Path of Least Resistance (DMA)* or go to http://www.robertfritz.com/

Chapter 9: I Can Do This One Step At A Time

1. Stanislavski, C., *Creating a Role*, NEL Mentor Books, p.49 (1961)

2. See www.chickensoup.com

CONTACT DETAILS

To contact Dr Dina Glouberman, order her books and CDs, download MP3s of Imagework exercises, find out about courses and events, or set up workshops or speaking engagements, please go to: www.dinaglouberman.com.

If you have enjoyed this book, why not try Dr Dina Glouberman's classic bestsellers, *Life Choices, Life Changes: Develop Your Personal Vision with Imagework* and *Joy of Burnout: How the End of the World Can Be a New Beginning*.

Life Choices, Life Changes: Develop Your Personal Vision with Imagework is a practical guide to a multitude of ways you can use imagery to understand and guide your life, from work to relationships to health to time and money to living a long and happy life. It is a classic textbook for anyone interested in working with imagery personally or professionally, yet written in very simple language. There is a CD and MP3 series to take you through the exercises in the book.

Joy of Burnout: How the End of the World Can Be a New Beginning is a groundbreaking study of why people burn out, how to recognize it, what to do about it, and how to head it off or minimize its impact. Above all, it reframes burnout positively as a step on your soul journey. Not to be missed if you or anyone you know is burning out, burnt out or about to burn out.

Both of these books are available from the website at

http://www.dinaglouberman.com/shop/ or alternatively from Amazon.co.uk or Amazon.com. CDs and MP3s are available only from http://www.dinaglouberman.com/shop/#cd-list

If you would like a brochure for Skyros Holidays, the world leader in holistic holidays, co-founded by Dina Glouberman, go to www.skyros.com or email office@skyros.com.